What would push you to *your*

Vanishing Point...?

by Colin Saxo

This is entirely a work of fiction. Names, characters and events are from the author's imagination. The representation of any real event or person in a description, photograph or otherwise is purely coincidental and intended without any intention to embarrass or cause offence.

Readers' reviews of *Vanishing Point*

Brilliant...

AC, UK

So good!

VL, UK

Gripping, I wanted to keep reading to find out what was happening...

SD, England

Enjoying this...

RC, New Zealand

I want to know why she's running away.

MR, UK

Thank you to all those who convinced me to start writing.

To Emma

Contents

Part One   A Dilemma 14

   Escape! 16

   Lying low 21

   Camouflage 27

   Disguise 38

   Confusion 46

   Restrictions 52

   Official stuff 58

   Interview 65

   New start 72

   Calling for help 80

Part 2   A Fresh Start 86

   Working woman 88

   Independence 94

   Freedom 104

   Shadows 111

   Contact 117

   Secrets 123

   Knowledge 127

Some answers 134

Next steps... 146

Quick progress... 155

Part 3 Big Changes 164

Reconnecting 166

Testing times 176

Worries 185

Celebrations 195

Results 202

Serious decisions... 207

Moving on... 217

Getting better... 224

Going forward 234

Part One   A Dilemma

Escape!

I pulled my hood up and walked quickly towards the main road. The drizzle increased as I plunged my hands into my coat pockets and pulled it closer to me. Feeling the warmth of my arms across me helped me feel the strength I needed to continue towards the openness of the dual carriageway. Unused to being alone, I felt the space around me both support and smother at the same time, as it gradually wrapped around me. My pace quickened as the traffic noise grew, the lights of the cars flashed as they drove across the end of the avenue. My shoulder bag bumped against my hip as I hastened my pace again. The corner approached and, as I turned onto the main road, I glanced over my shoulder along the avenue I had just left. I saw the outline of two men, walking quickly about fifty yards behind me. My heart beat faster as I looked ahead, towards the traffic lights which announced the presence of a further challenge. I needed to cross this road. Four lanes of traffic prevented me from reaching the trees on the other side, the line of oak trees bordering the town's parkland where acres of grass allowed freedom of movement to so many. I had spent hours there before, many hours of freedom, running around with my brothers, sisters and cousins whilst my mother and her sisters strolled across the openness as we all walked to the high street to accomplish the day's task of food shopping. Walking slowly across the stretch of soft grass allowed the adults to chat and the young members of the group to run, to shout and to hide behind bushes and trees to be discovered by the other children. Delighted shouts announced the appearance of those seeking, and startled shrieks from those who had thought they were hiding!

The strident beeping of the pelican crossing announced the safety of passage across the road, breaking into a run I covered the last few yards of pavement and I stepped into the road. Running to the small square of raised tarmac in the middle of the road, I paused and looked the other way at the two cars sitting side by side. I could see the driver of one reaching for the gear shift as the beeping stopped. My heart missed a beat as I recognised the face of the man driving, and the lady beside him looked right at me. I sprinted across the road as the cars began to move forward, the other car with unknown occupants honked its horn as it accelerated across my recent path. I turned and ran alongside the road. I ran and ran, towards the oncoming traffic, with the trees on my left and speeding cars on my right. They began to slow down as the beeping began again. Knowing that more pedestrians would be crossing, I ran as fast as I could to the next tree and pressed myself against the trunk. Gasping as the evening air forced itself into my chest, tasting the faint fumes from the cars I peered round the trunk to the footpath at the crossing. The two men I had glimpsed were hurrying towards the trees, I quickly grabbed the strap of my bag and ran across the grass. Away from the trees, away from the road, running, running, running for my life...

The words echoed in my head; I had seen them printed on the spine of a book in the supermarket on one of my trips to secure the ingredients for a Sunday meal. Looking for turnips and carrots had been my task, and the words had come into my vision as I passed a promotional stand at the end of an aisle. Run For Your Life. I ran faster and faster, my dress rustled and bundled itself beneath my thick coat as the drizzle mixed with sweat on my face. 'Run, run. Run, run...' The word repeated in time with my feet hitting the ground as I sprinted towards the high street. There would be some shops there, maybe one or two might still be open, although the crowds would have gone by now as it was about eight o'clock, everyone would have gone home. I ran with my heartbeat thudding in my ears. My hood fell back as I ran through the gloom towards the lights.

I looked back, quickly, and could see two figures hurrying behind me. They slipped slightly in the mud, they would be wearing their smart shoes, with expensive leather soles, whereas I had on my flat shoes with a thicker tread, less likely to slip in the mud or on wet roads. I think these may have given me away at the last minute, as they were not the usual shoes I would wear to a meeting, and someone may have noticed and reported me, but I couldn't have done otherwise. I was nearing the trees which bounded the park from the shopping side. I knew I would have to run to another crossing as the traffic on this main road was even heavier than the previous one. The winking amber lights showed through the trees, and I raced towards them. The mud splashed up around my feet and my face ran with a mixture of drizzle, sweat and unwanted tears. I reached the trees and swung myself around onto the footpath - glancing behind the trees to the gloom of the grassland I could see the figures, still running after me. I ran to the crossing and pressed the button, sobbing. I hammered the touch pad in a vain attempt to hurry the red light to stop the traffic.

'Pointless!' snapped a voice, 'It won't make it work more quickly!'

I kept my head down, my chest heaved as I tried to stifle the sobs and catch my breath; all I could see of the voice's owner was a pair of smart, black shoes and dark blue trouser legs. The voice was a lady's voice, and she was wearing trousers. The traffic slowed and the lights changed. Again, I ran across the two lanes, then the second set of lanes - and I ran. Ran towards the shops with lights on. I looked around as the traffic began. One man was just reaching the crossing and his attempt to cross the road was foiled. I could see the frustration in his stance as he clenched his fists and flung his head back.

'There...' he shouted and pointed towards me. He was looking across the road. The second man had overtaken him and had reached my side of the road and was about thirty yards from me. Terror filled me as I tried to run faster, although faster was a relative term, I was exhausted. Tears poured down my face as I turned to face the end of the chase... But the second man was still at the crossing. The snappy lady in trousers was holding his arm and speaking at his face. He was pulling away from her, but she was holding on tightly. I could see her leaning backwards slightly as he tried to slacken her firm hold on his sleeve. He pulled harder, trying to loosen her grip, and she stepped reluctantly towards him. The beeping started again, and I knew that the other man would soon join the tussle, so I took the chance given and ran again. I ran in front of the glowing shop windows and towards a welcome open door. A large household supplies shop enveloped me, and I remembered it from the many visits to buy cleaning materials and vegetable seeds. I slowed down to a fast walk and made for the back door. To the car park. Past the forbidden shelves of makeup and perfume, past the unpermitted items of scented candles and pet food, towards the stairs behind the row of checkouts. I dashed up the steps, out through the automatic doors that swished shut behind me and I ran again through the small car parking area behind the store. Along the linking footpath to the main town car park where I searched for the red beret which I knew would show that my rescuer was there. The car park lighting wasn't as clear as the streetlights had been, and I looked around wildly for the bright colour as the sobs rose again. There! There it was! I ran towards it and its wearer turned as I got closer. She glanced at my face, muddied, tear stained and wet.

'Were you seen?'

I nodded. Clutching my bag, I allowed her to grab my arm.

'Quickly!'

We both hurried as she pushed me towards a grey vehicle. A driver was already in the car, and I heard the engine start as we approached. My instinct forced me to stop at the side of the car.

Red beret lady opened the back door, 'Get in... Get IN!'

She pushed me through the door and a short scream escaped from me as she slammed the door.

'It's OK, it's OK.' Another voice, from the driver this time, reassured me.

The lady got into the car, and it began to move before the door had closed. She twisted in her seat and grabbed my hand.

'It's OK. Stay down. Stay down...' As the car drove towards the entrance to the main road, I could see people in dark clothing. I ducked down behind the front seats, taking huge, shuddering breaths and wiping my streaming face on my sleeve. The car crawled along past the stationary vehicles, quiet as they awaited their human cargo, past the people returning to their homeward transportation, and I began to breathe more slowly. The car turned and accelerated along the shopping street. Towards, well, I didn't know. But it had to be better. A future.

Lying low

I opened my eyes and gazed at the unfamiliar ceiling. Stripes of daylight alternated with shadow, and I turned towards the window, which was covered with a slatted blind, not the usual grey curtains that had protected my bedroom from the early morning sunshine for almost twenty years. The walls around the window glowed a pale peachy colour, the familiar white paint was only on the ceiling, behind the striped shadows. I sat up and looked around me. Pictures of mountains and lakes hung on the wall opposite the bed, the bed was huge, as big as my parents' bed, and covered in a patterned covered quilt. My blankets were nowhere to be seen. I looked at my hands, pressing down on the quilt, they looked red, and my arms shook slightly. I took a deep breath and let it out slowly as I looked further around the room. I saw, on a chair beyond the end of the bed, my dress. Dark green, and with long sleeves, it was warm and cosy and comfortable. I could see the mud around the hem, dried to a pale brown. My shoulder bag lay on the floor beside the nightstand, and I reached sideways to rummage among the few things I had been able to bring with me. I found clean underclothes and, pushing the quilt away, stood up to change out of yesterday's underwear which had doubled as nightwear. To have brought my usual nightgown would have filled my shoulder bag too much and made me too noticeable. I pulled my dress over my head and combed my fingers through my hair. Sliding my headband on I opened the door, wondering if there was a lavatory nearby. An open door opposite my room indicated that it was a bathroom, so I went in and made use of the facilities, washing my face with my hands. A bright yellow towel hung on a rail, and I pressed my face into it. The soft fabric smelt of honeysuckle. I breathed it in, and again. Replacing the towel,

I opened the door and went down the stairs, walking quickly by a window as I reached the top of the stairs. I could hear voices as I trod down the steps, I couldn't make out the conversation, but then a door opened and I gasped - the red beret lady appeared and looked up at me, I was still on the stairs, holding the banister.

'Good morning, would you like some breakfast?' She smiled and stepped across the small hallway towards another door. Pushing it open she entered and reached towards an electric kettle. She flicked the switch as I followed her in, and she turned towards me. 'What would you like me to call you? You can call me Libby.'

'Um, my name is...'

'No, we usually suggest a different one, for now.'

'Oh, well, um, let's say... '. I couldn't think of any name, I looked around the room, some books lay on the counter, Mary. That would do. 'Mary. Yes. Mary.' I looked at Libby and smiled.

She had followed my gaze and smiled too. 'Good choice. Mary it is. Now, breakfast!' She indicated a small table with chairs. I sat down in front of a toaster and an orange fruit bowl filled with grapes and bananas. A wooden storage container engraved with the word Bread stood on one side of the toaster, and a small tray containing jars of jam and marmalade with supermarket labels on the other. Libby brought over a mug of tea and a ceramic butter dish. Placing both on the table, she reached in a cupboard and handed me a plate. Then a butter knife and some teaspoons. 'Help yourself, there are croissants in the bread box too.'

I hesitated, I wasn't used to just sitting down in front of food and eating immediately. Libby pulled out the other chair and sat down too. She looked at me and said that I didn't have to do anything I didn't want to, so I closed my eyes and paused, then opened them and lifted the lid of the bread box.

We ate and drank in silence; my mind was racing. What was happening? What had I done? Where should I be? What was next? Libby slid a leaflet over to me. 'We can talk whenever you want to, about anything, but this might help.'

I read the words on the front of the leaflet. 'A Fresh Start. For those who are changing their lives for the better.'

I turned the page and saw pictures of fields and cattle. A woman driving a tractor. The next page showed people driving vans, and standing in a semicircle in a yard, all smiling. The accompanying text described a range of occupations, and a list of telephone numbers. Another page headed FAQs listed some questions. *'What do I wear? Where do I get my food? How can I pay for things? Who can I trust?'* I looked up at Libby again. 'I don't know what to do now.'

'We can do whatever you like, maybe the first thing is to get you some clothes, some people want to cut their hair... What would be the first thing you would like to do? We can do more or less anything!'

'Yes, I think some clothes would be a good idea, but where do we get them from? Is it safe?'

'We are about twelve miles from where we met last night, we can go to the next town, it's got one of those hospice support shops, a couple of chain stores and a supermarket. Nothing very fancy, but it's a good place to start. There is a hairdresser too. We can call in there if you like. It should be safe, I've never seen any of them there, but we will keep an eye out. I'll drive us and we can use the

Fund to pay. You're given five hundred pounds to change your style, I'm guessing you didn't bring much with you?'

'I've got two spare sets of underclothes with me.'

'Right, well, we'll get some more of those then! I'm thinking some jeans, a couple of t-shirts, some pyjamas and a jumper or fleece as well as underwear. And some socks and trainers too.'

I laughed. Jeans! Never had I wore jeans! The possibility was far too remote to be considered. I began to relax a bit. This could be a good day!

I stood up and approached the sink, taking my plate and mug to wash. Libby handed me a bulging drawstring bag made from an orange and red patterned fabric.

'This is your welcome pack, just some essentials. Obviously, everything in the house is for your use, but you might like your own personal stuff.'

I pulled at the cords holding the bag closed and peered inside; the fabric was of a thick, slightly shiny waterproof type so I was unable to see the contents properly. I emptied the bag onto the newly cleared table, a wrapped bar of soap thudded onto the wooden tabletop, a couple of packets of sanitary pads, and a small box of tampons followed. I'd never seen those outside a shop, they were forbidden in the Community. A slim cardboard box containing a toothbrush, a tube of toothpaste, a flat plastic packet with plastic sticks of some sort inside, a hairbrush, a lipstick and a small glass bottle also fell out, and I shook the bag again as something made of fabric slid slowly out. A brightly printed silky scarf opened itself and fluttered down, covering the packets and the brush... 'Oh! This is beautiful!' I picked it up and threaded it through my hands. Every shade of blue and green twisted around my fingers.

'It's a print of Monet's, the painter. As soon as I saw how blue your eyes are I thought it will go well with your colouring.'

I smiled and offered thanks before returning everything back into the bag, intending to take it back upstairs to the bathroom; I walked past the door where conversation continued in the room beyond. I looked in, expecting to see more people, but it was a television. The bright screen showed two smartly dressed people talking and gesticulating over a large map of the country. Rain was mentioned, and pictures of clouds came and went. Libby appeared again. 'It should stay fine this morning, we can go whenever you like, but maybe sooner rather than later?'

I continued watching the people. The screen changed, music played and suddenly a woman appeared, holding a bottle of cleaning fluid that I had seen in the shops.

'Oh, I wish they wouldn't do that,' said Libby as she crossed the room, she picked up a flat black box and held it in front of her. 'It's so sexist!'

I stared at her, shocked. 'What's sexist?' I could feel my face getting hot and pressed my hand to my cheek. The screen had changed to black now, and a red dot glowed in the frame.

'That they show women doing the cleaning and have them extolling the most expensive cleaning fluid available. We're facing a planetary crisis, with pollution at crazy levels, yet they suggest that a woman should only focus on intensifying the problem. And from the kitchen too. Have the suffragettes made so little impact?'

I stared at Libby in confusion. What did she mean? Planetary crisis? Pollution? And what was a suffragette? What was it supposed to have impacted upon?

Confusion filled my head as I went back to the bathroom. Those words I had never heard before ricocheted around, but the one that really worried me was the one about sex. Sexist sounded insistent. What was this house? Where was the driver from yesterday? He had dropped us off and driven away in the grey car. Was he something to do with the sexist? I brushed my teeth, and then my hair. I looked in the mirror and remembered my new lipstick. I'd look at that later. The sexist was still worrying me. I went back downstairs, where Libby was picking up a small red leather bag. A much smaller version of my own brown canvas shoulder bag. I had left that upstairs by the bed I had slept so soundly in, and had tried to make tidy before leaving, as was my usual routine. I hadn't been able to tuck the bedclothes in properly, the corners hadn't worked and there wasn't a bedspread. But I had tried, and it looked smooth.

'Ready?' asked Libby.

I nodded, still pondering the flurry of new words. I picked up my coat, followed her outside, and waited as she pressed buttons beside the front door, then a beeping noise sounded as she locked the front door and led me over to a small blue car. Orange lights flashed and a click sounded. She opened the driver's door, and I opened the back door.

'No, Mary, sit by me in the front...'

Camouflage

Sitting in the passenger seat now, beside Libby, I looked at the trees and fields as they flew past the window of the car. 'Where are we? Or aren't I supposed to know?'

'Of course, you can know, you aren't kidnapped...! We're just coming up to Market Wenton.'

'It's because of the Mary business. I wasn't sure. It's all a bit confusing.'

'Oh, I see. No, the name thing is in case we need to call to each other for any reason, your appearance will be different, but you will probably still be recognisable, especially if your name is the same. Using a different name provides a distraction in case someone thinks they do recognise you. It's best to use that name all the time so I don't make a mistake and call you by your real one, which would give the game away! The jeans will make a big difference, as they are the opposite of what you wear normally. And if we change your hair that will make a big difference too. What do you think about that?'

'Yes, let's do that. I'm not going back, so let's change it!' I reached behind my head and gathered my hair into a forbidden ponytail, I slid one hand along the full length of my hair, it must be almost two feet long. What should I do? How much could I change it?

The car was slowing down a bit, the fields were beginning to contain houses, then the houses were closer together, then stuck together, with no gaps between them. I remembered my own home, set in a large lawned garden, it was nearer in appearance to the houses we had seen on the outskirts of this town. We had neighbours, but we waved to them, we didn't look upon them from arm's length as we left our respective front doors. My father had built a wall around our property, gradually replacing the fence panels as they had rotted, the wall growing by several meters a year until it fully enclosed our garden. I had loved the garden, it had a whole area of fruit growing, I had loved to pick the raspberries when they grew late in the summer. We had grown a lot of our own vegetables, my mother had shown me how to grow different sorts of beans, and peas too. Digging the bean trench had been the first job of the year, as soon as the frosts had ended, I was out there with a spade, digging industriously, my wellingtons caking in the clay soil that made up most of the garden. I had always got quite muddy as my dresses had stuck to the sides of the trench as it deepened, and to the sides of my wellingtons. Mother had only scolded me sometimes though, she knew how hard it was to dig, but she also seemed to be forever washing clothes and pegging them onto a spinning line. It hadn't ever spun much, it creaked as it swung jerkily around in the wind... My eyes filled with tears as I thought of my home. I wouldn't see it again, I knew that. And neither would I see my family. I rubbed away a tear as it slid down to my chin. Libby noticed as she turned into a car park. We paused at a barrier, then it rose, and we drove underneath then past signs with ANPR on them and descriptions of payment methods. She parked the car and sat still for a moment.

'I know this is hard for you Mary,' she said as she reached for my hand. I let her take it in hers and she squeezed it gently. 'We can stop whenever you like, but I think it's important not to go backwards. We can wait until you feel like going on. Ask me anything, anything at all, whenever you need to. I'll answer you or find out an answer. I've helped other people, and it's different for everyone. I think I have heard everything, then I meet someone new, and I hear something else. I'm unshockable, so don't hesitate to talk to me. At any time.'

'I know. There's so much I want to ask, but I really want to know what's the sexist. It sounds scary. And sinister.'

She looked at me, and started to speak, then stopped and looked ahead. Thinking. Then she turned and said,

'It's a way of describing something that should only be done by a woman, or only done by a man, rather than something being done by either a man or a woman. Like that cleaning advert on the telly, it's sexist to suggest that cleaning should only be done by a woman. Or cooking should only be done by a woman. It's sexist to say that only a man should be a train driver, or that women shouldn't play football. It's a form of discrimination, and it's illegal. We should allow men and women to do everything, there are no jobs or activities that are banned for one sex. It's nothing to do with having sex.'

My face felt hot again, and I pressed my free hand to my cheek.

'I'm sorry, Mary, I'm not trying to shock you.'

'I don't think I'm shocked, it's just we were never allowed to say the word, and I've never heard of Sexist. I'm sure I'll have to adapt to a lot of things, and there are lots of words I want to understand.'

'I can imagine. Are you OK to go shopping? Or shall we take five minutes?'

I took a deep breath. 'I'm fine. Let's go!'

We left the car, with more flashing of the lights and clicking, and walked out of the car park towards the shopping street. We went past different shops, a grooming parlour for dogs, a nail bar - whatever that was - some clothing shops that didn't seem to be the ones that Libby had in mind, then a brightly lit shop with lots of clothes racks. I followed her in, I had only ever been to one or two fairly dingy shops before, one selling second hand dresses and cardigans. If I'd wanted underclothes, I had gone to the general store further down the shopping street. But this shop that I was in with Libby was huge, with racks and racks of clothes. Statues stood by the windows, with brightly coloured clothes in unusual shapes pinned to them. More statues were standing inside the main part of the shop, some of them in very little clothing indeed. Libby was standing by a table covered in piles of blue jeans. 'What would you like? Boot cut? Skinny? Straight? Low rise? On the waist? What size are you?'

'I have no idea what you are talking about!'

Libby laughed, and turned over a pile, picking out a pair from the bottom, then flicking down another pile and sliding out another one. She passed them to me, then led me over to an area where the shelves were stacked with brightly coloured t-shirts, and sort of half-statues, the top halves, were arranged on the top of the shelves. The statues were each wearing a different style of t-shirts. I hadn't known that there could be so many different shapes, necklines or sleeve lengths but it seemed that absolutely anything was possible. I felt the fabric, stroking it with my thumb. It was so soft, and the colours were so bright. Libby continued to ask me questions, which colours did I prefer? What shape did I like? I blinked at her in confusion, and she laughed again. She took two pink ones, and two striped in navy and white, and two white ones. Handing them to me, she took me over to a lady standing by an archway.

'We've got eight!' The lady pressed a button, and handed her a large plastic disc.

'Cubicle seven...'

I followed Libby to a row of what could be public lavatory doors. The one with 7 on the door was empty and I went in. Closing the door, I hung up the t-shirts, placed the jeans on the stool in the corner and flicked off my shoes. I pulled my mud-stained dress over my head and hung it on the spare hook beside the bright t-shirts. I stepped into the jeans and slid them up my legs. I pulled them up, feeling the fabric around my thighs. There was a button and a zip, and I did them both up. I pulled on a t-shirt and hauled my long hair up out of the back of the t-shirt before I looked at myself in the mirror. The cool cotton of the t-shirt felt a little like my now abandoned nightgown. I smoothed it over my stomach and heard Libby calling through the door.

'Mary? How are you getting on? Can you show me?'

I opened the door and faced her. She looked at the jeans, then the t-shirt.

'The jeans look a bit big, are they the 14? And the t-shirt looks a bit tight. Try the size twelve jeans, and the other pink t-shirt.'

Obediently, I closed the door and changed the clothes as Libby had suggested. I opened the door again.

'Much better! Try the other t-shirts, the size twelves. I think the tens will be too small.'

I looked at the hangers and saw that there were little plastic cubes at the base of each hook, the pink ones had 10 printed on them, the green ones had 12. I picked up the twelves and slid them off the hangers. Again, I closed the door. Five minutes later I was wearing my familiar heavy dress as we handed the t-shirts with the 10 cubes, and the jeans with blue 14 cubes to the lady by the archway. She smiled and thanked Libby and Libby thanked her. There seemed to be a lot of talking that went on in this new world I was in! I followed Libby as she walked between the racks of clothes to a smaller section at the back of the shop. Suddenly we were surrounded by underwear. My face felt hot again, and Libby saw my embarrassment. She walked over to where some plastic packets hung up with the little cubes on the hooks again and handed me one of them. 'Do you like these? We can get different ones if you prefer...'

I nodded and took the packet. There were five different colours of rolled up fabric, and Bikini Multipack was printed across the front. Already Libby was reaching up by another rack. This time of what looked like short t-shirts. She handed me a white one, a fawn coloured one and a black one. The little green cubes clattered as she turned to me. 'Do you want to try these on? I'm guessing you don't know your cup size...'

More strange words. What did cups have to do with t-shirts? I looked at her in confusion. She had already turned away and was walking over to where there were hundreds of socks. In every colour imaginable. She picked up another packet and I followed her as we returned to the archway. This time I noticed a sign glowing above the archway, Fitting Rooms. I smiled at the lady and Libby showed her the t-shirts. Again, she pressed a button and handed her a plastic disc. 'Cubicle four please.'

I closed the door and again took off my dress. I pulled on the t-shirt and looked in the mirror stuck to the back of the door. It looked a bit strange, there seemed to be too much material and it was a bit tight. I opened the door a little and peered round the edge. I whispered to Libby, 'It's too tight...'

She put her hand on the door and I pushed it against the pressure of her hand.

'I've not got my dress on...'

'Oh, I see. Just a minute...' She went away and I closed the door.

She came back almost immediately and knocked...

'Mary, put this on...' I opened the door, and she slid in a purple skirt on a hanger.

'I don't need a skirt,'

'No, but if you put that on, maybe you would be comfortable showing me your top half?'

'Oh, yes.'

A moment later I opened the door and Libby looked in. The skirt made me decent, and the t-shirt was still a bit strange. Libby tilted her head.

'Maybe take them both off, and then try the white one on again on its own. It's for wearing under a t-shirt, it's a bralette.'

'Oh!!!' My face felt hot again as I closed the door. How stupid I was.

Opening the door again, my face was still hot, but at least I was dressed correctly. The top that Libby had chosen looked much better without my vest underneath it, it clung to my chest, and I could see that I had an outline like the statues I had been looking at a few minutes earlier. Libby had handed me the pink t-shirt I had tried on a few minutes earlier and I had put it on top. It looked amazing. I really did look like the statues. I looked at Libby and she smiled. I smiled back and my face didn't feel hot anymore.

'Better? You look fabulous!'

'Better.' I said and closed the door again.

Standing in the checkout queue a few minutes later, I had my new jeans, a blue jumper we had picked up on the way from the changing rooms; Libby called it a teal sweater, which reminded me of a bird, but it looked lovely near my face as it toned well with the blue in my eyes and felt quite soft, my t-shirts and what I now knew to be my new underwear in a big bundle in my arms when Libby told me to stay there and she rushed off. My heart began to beat faster, and I could hear my ears swishing as my breath became faster. Where was she going? I looked round in a panic and tried to call her. My mouth was dry, and I couldn't speak. I looked wildly round and saw her running back to me... She squeezed past the people standing behind me, the man closest to me was beginning to gaze at me quite intently and I swallowed hard. My arms were beginning to tremble, and tears were close. She arrived beside me and said I'd better have the jeans in black too. She looked at me and saw my trembling lip and her eyes widened.

'Oh god, sorry Mary. I'm so stupid, I should have thought...'

We shuffled further forward in the queue and the tears receded as my heartbeat slowed. The man behind me lost interest and started to pat his pockets as a strident bell sounded. I had seen this happen before; it was likely to be a phone call. The phone at our house stood on a table, in the hallway at the bottom of the staircase. It was not used often, but occasionally it rang with a tinkling sound, and Mother would run to answer it if my father wasn't home. If he was, then he spoke first. I heard the man silence the noise then answer, 'Hey, Max!'

None of the politeness shown at home, 'Good Afternoon' were always the first words spoken, the telephone rarely rang and only occasionally calls were made. I had watched my mother turn the circular disc, she had put her finger into a hole above a number and pushed the disc around until it rested against a silver bar, then withdrew her finger to allow the disc to return. A quiet clicking noise had sounded until the disc came to rest, when she had repeated the process for the next number. Eventually she had stood and waited until a faint voice said 'Hello?' and she had spoken the message she had been tasked with. At no time were we children permitted to even touch the telephone, far less make a call, or answer one. There were six of us all together, my oldest brother was almost a man, he would be regarded as such as soon as he was married. I knew that he was waiting for a match to be made for him, he would move into his own house then, and that wouldn't be far off, he was now twenty-two and that was old enough. His wife was likely to be a few years younger, as my oldest sister had been married for just over a year and she was twenty-one. I knew that my marriage would be being arranged as I would be twenty soon, and girls usually married at that age. I had another sister, at twenty she was almost a year older than I, and she was expected to marry very soon. That left a younger brother, he was seventeen, then another sister, I called her my blonde sister as she had blonde hair and all the rest of us had black hair. My father had black hair, although it was growing grey above his ears. My mother had brown hair, very dark brown, but she too was going grey, underneath her headband it was difficult to see the hair growing above her ears, but there were quite thick stripes of grey in the hair falling from her hairband down her back to her hips.

There was another child, a sister, she had something wrong with her, and my mother used to push her in a bigger than normal pushchair if she had to take her out. She hardly ever left the house, staying in her bed or, if the weather was fine, she lay on a blanket in the garden. My mother didn't talk to her much, I don't know what she had done to deserve such a punishment and we others were all kept away from her when I had lived at the house, especially my brothers. My mother spooned sloppy food into her mouth after we had all eaten, mashing up what was left in the serving dishes. My other sisters and I washed the dishes and replaced them on the shelves inside the big cupboard beside the long table where we all ate together. Long benches either side of the table meant that we could accommodate more people when it had been our turn to cook the main lunch - Father had a big chair at one end, of course, and there were three more big chairs for the other men who had attended the lunches. They stayed pushed against the wall until they had been needed, and we had kept them clean and polished.

I returned to the present suddenly, as Libby nudged me. It was our turn. I followed Libby to the cash desk and put down my unstable bundle of clothes. The assistant started to scan the tags attached to each garment, and Libby pulled a couple of folded carrier bags out of her red shoulder bag, and a wallet. She opened the wallet and slid a brightly coloured plastic card from the slots inside. She put the clothes into the bags, as the assistant scanned the underwear. My face felt hot again as I wondered if other people could see, but then they were in the bag and the card was pushed into the reader and the little machine handed to Libby, she pressed a few buttons, then paused, when the machine beeped it was handed back to the assistant and she removed the card and a strip of paper twirled its way out of the machine before being torn off and handed back to Libby along with the bright plastic card. More gratitude was expressed as we thanked each other in turn, and with the assistant's wish that we had a nice 'rest of your day' we left the shop holding a bag each. The shopping continued in two more shops, where we bought a pair of shoes, or 'trainers' as Libby referred to them, and a jacket. I could see my distinctive coat was to be redundant! Then we paused in front of a different shop. A haircutters'. I looked through the window. This would be the most significant part of my transformation. My long hair was noticeable, and not many women had such long hair. Community women were not allowed to cut or style their hair, attention to personal appearance was regarded as vanity and make up was disapproved of for the same reason. Some of the older ladies would twist their long hair into a sort of knot, but anything more brought severe disapproval. Hair should be covered by a plain headscarf or a wide headband, so standing on the threshold of this shop felt very exciting. Libby looked at me. 'What do you think?' I smiled broadly, nodded and pushed open the door.

Disguise

Libby followed me in and asked if there was anyone free to do a cut and finish. More conversation followed, apparently, I was being made over! It all sounded a bit worrying, but Libby took my bag from me, and told me to take off my coat. The shop lady called to another girl who was standing towards the back of the room, stacking small boxes onto a shelf. 'Maria? Can you come and do this lady's hair please?'

Maria approached and I was surprised to see that when she turned her head her hair changed colour. When she remained still her hair was black, but when she moved, her hair swished and there was purple hair hidden beneath the black. I liked that. My own hair was black, but I wasn't sure if I wanted purple hair at this stage! I heard Libby suggesting to Maria that a shoulder length layered bob might work, Maria looked at me as I sat, wrapped in a slippery sheet like a shroud, in a shiny armchair and I nodded.

'It's a lot to cut off, what are your thoughts on donation? We could send it to Care to Shair?' Libby asked me if I wanted to keep my hair, or would I mind if it was used to help other people, people who had had something called keymoh and needed a wig. I had no idea what she meant by any of that, but, as I didn't want my hair, I said it would be fine to donate it. Why anyone would want to have someone else's hair I couldn't imagine, but I certainly didn't want it.

Maria handed me my headband and started on my hair. She plaited it into a rope down my back, and then produced some scissors. I nodded my agreement when she asked if I was really sure, and I heard the rasp of the scissors as they cut through my hair. It took Maria some time to cut all the way through, but suddenly I felt a lightness and the rope fell to the floor. She picked up the rope and handed it to the first lady who took it away through a door at the back of the shop. Maria asked me to follow her to a backwash. Confused, I followed her. A backwash sounded like something to do with a boat, but she stopped after a few steps and indicated a chair with a bowl behind it and a spray handle inside the bowl. I sat down and swiftly found myself leaning backwards over the bowl as she washed my hair. I was beginning to understand a little more, she rubbed at my hair with shampoo which smelt of coconuts.

My mother had once used a lotion with coconut oil on my poor sister's sore skin and the smell was so memorable. After more washing and rubbing and washing I was sitting back in front of the mirror whilst Maria rubbed at my hair with a thick black towel. I had never felt so free, my long, long hair had always taken ages to wash, we had done that on a Saturday, all of us girls at once, rubbing each other's hair dry with a thin towel. Then sitting and combing each other's hair, one behind the other almost in a circle. There were four of us all together, as my poor sister didn't have her hair washed very often, and wasn't capable of holding a comb anyway, I know my mother washed it from time to time, but it wasn't done in the same routine as my other sisters and me. I liked my younger sister to comb my hair for me; the others were a little impatient and tugged rather. I tried not to tug with the comb, but it was hard as it took so long to do. The memories of this weekly task filled my thoughts as Maria snipped around my face and shoulders. Then she clattered around to one side of me and flicked a switch on a big cone on a stick; a whoosh of hot air hit my ear. I jumped and a squeak escaped from me!

Libby smiled at me through the mirror, from her chair behind me she had seen everything, and her reassuring smile helped me to relax a bit as Maria pointed the hot air around my hair, all the while winding a spiky brush through my hair and stretching it to the end of my now much, much shorter hair. Suddenly she stopped brushing, switched off the air, and flicked through my hair, scooping it back from my face and running her fingers through it. Stepping back, she smiled at me and asked what I thought. I looked at my face. I looked so different. My hair no longer stretched my forehead backwards, the tugging at my temples had gone; instead, black fluffy hair floated around my cheeks and beside my chin. I smiled and could hardly recognise the face looking at me.

The mirror at home had been old and it hung in the hallway as part of the coat stand. We looked at ourselves to check we wouldn't shame our parents as we left the house. My brothers never looked, but we girls had to check our hairbands were positioned properly. They matched the colour of our hair, we all had black hair, apart from my younger sister, whose hair was blonde. Her hairbands were easy to find, the creamy colour stood out against the dark furniture and floorboards. The rest of us shared the black hairbands, it didn't matter that we didn't have our own, we had so few individual possessions anyway.

I realised I still had my hairband in my hand. I shoved it into the pocket of my dress and resolved not to wear it again. Maria reached around to the front of my shroud and undid the bow holding it around me. She stepped back and I stood up. Seeing myself in the thick, dark dress without the thick, dark hair looked a little strange. Libby had fetched my coat, still with the muddied hem, and dropped it on the floor as she rummaged in the bags, she pulled out my new jacket and held it for me as I stood awkwardly in front of her.

I took it from her and slid my arms in, one at a time. She reached forward and adjusted it across my shoulders. What a strange time I was having. I'd had my head rubbed, my hair cut off, a coat held for me, and four big carrier bags of shopping done for me. And none of the shopping was food! I suddenly realised I was hungry. Libby was once again at the cash desk, pushing the brightly coloured plastic card into yet another card reader, and accepting another slip of paper as a receipt. I realised that I would have to thank everyone again, as Libby was already thanking the first lady, and then Maria. I joined in and they thanked me too. The first lady handed me a leaflet about Care to Shair, it stated that it was a wig-making business for people who had lost their hair due to illness or treatment for cancer. I stared at it, cancer had never been mentioned in the Community – it was considered to be a punishment, to develop an illness like that, and another source of shame. I pushed it into my coat pocket before picking up two of the carrier bags that contained my new clothes, my old coat stuffed into the top of one of them, and we walked out of the shop, or salon as they had described it; Libby and I walked back to the car, exclaiming over how different my hair felt and looked. She opened the boot with more flashing lights and beeping, and we pushed the bags in alongside a box of items that Libby referred to as Junk. She reached into the box and felt about until she found a smaller plastic box, she opened it and took out a packet of chocolate bars. Handing two to me she said they would help until we got home, when we would eat. I could tell it was after lunchtime, I was used to stopping to eat at half past twelve, which had been my routine for about thirteen years – ever since I started going to the Community school, and getting into the car I could see on the dashboard clock that it was twenty past one. No wonder I was hungry! I sat beside Libby again as she drove us back to the house, as I ate my chocolate biscuit bar I listened as she spoke of my new image and suggested that I go upstairs to change as soon as we got home, whilst she made us some lunch and asked whether I liked omelettes. I assured her that I did, and I'd be glad to get changed, I was keen to take off the remaining link to my old life.

Soon we were back at the little house, it was half a house really, two homes in one building. Libby opened the door with her key and a sharp beeping sounded. She pressed some buttons on the wall beside the door and the beeping stopped. I could see a blue light flashing on the black machine on the shelf at the bottom of the stairs. Libby also noticed this and started to press more buttons as I went upstairs. I could hear an electronic voice announcing that 'There.... is.... ONE.... new.... message' and then a pause and a beep before a woman's voice said 'Libby, we're in a bit of trouble. The police have been and taken Hector in for questioning. Can you ring me back?' Libby gasped and pressed more buttons, and I heard the electronic voice again, this time listing numbers 'one, eight, four, four...' By now I was in my bedroom, tipping out my new clothes onto the bed, I changed into my blue jeans, and my pink t-shirt. I went downstairs to meet Libby who was whisking eggs in a jug.

'I can do that,' I said, 'I'm used to cooking, but usually I do it for at least eight of us.'

'Yes please, Mary,' said Libby. 'There could be a problem, Hector has been taken to the police station.'

'Who is Hector?' I asked as I poured some of the whisked eggs into a hot pan on the stovetop. The mixture bubbled and gradually slowed down to the required simmer as the eggs cooked. Grating some cheese to add to the mix, I listened as Libby explained that Hector was the man who had driven us here the night before.

'I can't imagine why he's gone to the police station; he is such a great bloke; he never even drives over the limit by one! I'm just ringing Sarah back; she left a message - although she didn't say much!' She was pressing a button on the machine on the shelf, which I now presumed to be a telephone, although there was neither curly wire, nor disc with circular holes above printed numbers. Instead, there were buttons on a rectangular pad, which wasn't tied to the machine at all. Like the man in the clothes shop's mobile phone really! I could hear the beeping of the handset, as she held it to her ear. Then a voice, 'Hello?'

'Sarah? It's Libby. What's happened?'

I continued to make the omelettes and put Libby's in front of her as she listened to Sarah. I ate mine as she asked a couple of questions in between mouthfuls. After saying goodbye to Sarah, she switched off the phone and turned her full attention to the rest of her omelette.

'Well, it seems that someone saw me pushing you into Hector's car last night and took the number of the car before reporting a suspected kidnapping to the police! Fabulous omelette, by the way, just as I like them. Thank you.'

'What will happen to Hector? Is he in trouble?'

'I don't think so, but we might have to talk to the police, to explain that we haven't kidnapped you.'

'What? ME? Talk to the police? Oh no...' I had been taught to stay away from any type of authority, the possibility of attracting attention to our Community was not a positive thing, and we were all brought up to do the right thing, to do nothing illegal, or anything that would attract attention. That I would be speaking to them personally was alarming. Would they take me away? I had always understood that if I left the Community, very bad things would happen, but so far, I had received nothing but kindness and friendliness. I decided to believe that the police would be kind too.

'Well, there's no point in looking for trouble, we will see what happens. We haven't done anything illegal, you wanted us to give you a lift here, and we did.

That's all. Unless your family have reported you as missing, there's no need to say any more. Do you think they will do that?'

'I don't know. I don't know if they would want me back for any other reason than to pretend that I never left, can they make me go back? The police I mean?'

'No, I don't think so. You are over 18 and therefore an adult. Your family may want you back, but are no longer legally responsible for you, so I think that they can report you missing, and if the police find you, they can let your parents know that you are alive and well but don't want to be in touch with anyone. It's entirely up to you. You can always go back if you want to, I'm not forcing you to stay if you do want to leave. If you want to continue with the escape, I'm here to support you, and haven't we done a good job so far?'

I looked at myself in the reflective front of the oven which was, for some reason, halfway up the wall. I looked nothing like the person I had been when I arrived less than a day ago. Would anyone from my old life recognise me? I think my face was still recognisable, I'd have to think about what to do. Maybe some make up? I had no idea about make up; it hadn't been allowed. 'How can I change my face, Libby? I think I look very different, but I want to be as certain as I can be.'

'You can wear some lipstick? And maybe some glasses with fairly heavy frames. They don't need to have proper lenses in, they won't affect how you see. I think your hair changes you quite a lot, and with glasses you will look very different. Did you see the lipstick from your bag this morning? Would you like to try that? I could show you?'

I went upstairs to fetch it. When I returned, Libby had got her own lipstick and was standing in front of the hall mirror. 'Let's do it together...' She pulled the lid off the lipstick and twisted it. A pink core appeared from the casing. I copied her. Pulling my lipstick in the same way, I removed the cap, then twisted until the core appeared. She turned the lipstick until the flat face of the point was facing her, I did the same. Opening her mouth in a gape, she stretched her lips into a smooth smile and drew the pink core from the centre of her top lip to the side. Then back to the centre and across to the other side. Then the bottom lip, again, from the centre to the side each time. She then pressed her lips together, sliding them slightly sideways and working the colour around a little bit until they were completely covered by the pink colour. I did the same, but I wasn't used to it and the effect was rather smudged.

'Never mind, wipe it off and try again. I'm used to it; I've worn it nearly every day for thirteen years. That's a lot of practice.'

I took the paper tissue she offered and wiped it all off. And tried again. And again... After a few more tries I turned to face her. 'What do you think?'

'That's looking great? Well done...!'

Behind me, there was a sudden loud knock on the door... We looked at each other. Then the knocking came again.

Confusion

Libby whispered that I should go upstairs, I complied quickly, and she opened the front door.

'Hello?'

'Good afternoon, may we speak to Ms Linton please?'

'That's me, I'm Libby.'

'Good afternoon, Libby; may we have a word? We are from Western Area Police and need to ask a few questions regarding a recent event.'

'May I see your ID please?'

'Yes....'

There was a pause, and some rustling, then Libby invited the people in, and she closed the door. I couldn't see them from where I was, sitting on my bed, but I heard them go into the room with the television. The door closed and I could hear voices but nothing like clear speech. Then the door opened, and Libby called up the stairs... 'Mary, have you got a minute to come down here please?'

I got off the bed and ran downstairs to where Libby was - she smiled and beckoned me into the front room. Two policemen sat on the sofa, both in black and bright yellow clothing. They both had short hair and one had a beard too. I followed Libby in, and we sat down on two chairs in front of the window.

'This is my friend Mary; she's staying with me for a while.' Libby introduced me briefly.

'Hello, Mary, my name is PC Thomas, and this is PC Singh. We have had reports of a possible kidnapping involving a grey Chrysler car yesterday evening. Initial investigations have led us to you and Libby here being passengers. What can you tell us about that?'

I blinked and looked at Libby. She nodded encouragingly, and I looked back at the policemen. 'I was in a grey car with Libby yesterday, yes. I haven't been kidnapped and there's nothing at all for anyone to worry about.' I smiled and looked at both policemen. They looked at me without smiling. They both had black blocks, about the size of a clenched fist clipped to their bright yellow jackets, also clipped on to their jackets was a sort of thick round disc which had a small, red flashing light. I had never been so close to a policeman and was a bit nervous. I was waiting to see what they were going to say; they looked at each other and the one with a beard asked me how long I had known Libby.

'Not very long at all, but she's my best friend.'

Libby smiled and squeezed my hand. The other policeman looked at her hand holding mine, then at Libby.

'What's the address of this house, Mary?'

'Pardon?' I was completely surprised.

'Where are we, Mary, what's your friend Libby's address...?' He looked intently at my face. My mouth opened and closed, and my face felt hot again. Libby had told me that I was blushing when I felt like this, so I knew that my face was red, which isn't a good sign as it suggested I was not comfortable. I remembered that Libby had said that we shouldn't say anything that wasn't true if the police asked us anything.

'I don't know the address, I telephoned to ask Libby if I could stay with her, and she arranged a lift to pick me up.'

'Why didn't you use your own car, Libby?'

Libby looked at the policeman and told him that she had had the offer of a lift from a friend and had accepted it. She looked at him steadily and he looked back, it was a long look, and I looked at the other policeman.

'Do you two ladies have ID please?'

The request surprised me, and I answered immediately. 'No.'

Libby spoke at the same time and reached for her red handbag.

'Yes, I have my driver's licence, here…' She reached across the room, and offered a pink plastic card to the policemen, one of them took it and looked carefully at it, turning it over and looking at her again. He handed it back.

'Thank you, Libby, you haven't got any ID Mary?'

'No, I didn't bring anything like that with me.'

He looked at me again. 'I see.'

The one without a beard stood up. 'Well, as no one has been kidnapped, we will get back to the station and write this up. We might be back in touch. Any holiday plans, ladies? Are you likely to be here if we need to talk some more?'

'No plans,' said Libby. 'We might go shopping or something, but we won't be far away.'

'Right.' Both policemen were standing up now, and Libby's little front room suddenly felt very crowded. They turned and walked to the front door. 'Many thanks, both. Take care!'

We sat in the front room and watched as the police car drove away. I thought about what had happened since yesterday afternoon. My world had absolutely changed for ever. The day-to-day routines for the last nineteen years had ended. I no longer had to go anywhere I didn't want to go to; I could speak if I wanted to, and I could have friends too. I looked at Libby and asked her what her life had been like.

'Well, Mary, not very different from yours to be honest, for the first fifteen years anyway. We lived about eighty miles away, in a town with a fairly large Community like yours. Then one day my father came in from work and said that we had to leave. In the same way that you left yesterday, we all left suddenly. Me, my parents and my two sisters. Possibly for the same reasons that you did. My older sister was eighteen and had finished school. She worked in the office of a business that supplied offices and other businesses with plants and was owned by a Community member. My father had been told that she should soon be getting married, and he couldn't face that. So, he decided that we should leave. He had been planning this for a while, since my grandparents had died a few years earlier. We didn't know at the time, but he had been trying to arrange for a new job for himself, and a new home for us all. We literally packed one bag each, got into the car and just drove away. That was thirteen years ago, and we closed the door on everything from that life. We don't see anyone from then, and we have made a much more contented life for us all. I'm twenty-eight now, and I couldn't be happier. I went to university; I've got a job and I've been dating. I've got a boyfriend and we are thinking of getting married. This is his house, and he is away at work at the moment. I'm a teacher, and I work in a local school during term time. In the school holidays I help out with the Network and that's how I was able to help you. It's the Easter holidays at the moment, and term starts again a week on Monday.'

So, Libby really did know how I felt. She understood.

'What happens now?'

'Well, the next step is to find your new life. The Network can help us, there are ways of making a completely fresh start, but you will have to be strong. You must decide not to go back at all. If you decide on a new life, it really shouldn't include anything from your old one. You already have a new name, and a new appearance. We can meet more people from the Network and work out where you would like to go. Do you know anyone else at all? On the Outside, I mean.'

'No. No-one at all.'

'That makes things easier, in a way. What was your job, before you left?'

'I didn't have one, I helped my mother in our house, and did cleaning and cooking in the houses of some of the older people.'

'Were you paid?'

'One couple paid me, they did it secretly, without anyone knowing. They told me to keep it safely, and it's in my bag upstairs. About two hundred pounds.'

'Right. Have you thought about what sort of job you would like to do?'

'I'm not sure. I don't know much, what sort of things can women do?'

'Well, we've seen several women working today, in the clothes shop and the hairdressers, but women can do anything. Join the army, be a police officer, a vet, a doctor, a lawyer. Anything. We just have to work out what you are good at, and whether you want to do that as a job. Let's have a look at that leaflet and see if anything grabs your attention.'

I unfolded the leaflet that Libby had given to me earlier and glanced down the lists of potential occupations. Nursing was a possibility, nannying, caring, housekeeping, gardening, animal care and other domestic roles which were compatible with the housework I had done within my home. Other topics were covered too, lots of telephone numbers of local authority offices that could advise on housing, how to get medical help, befriending groups and other sources of help for people who were literally starting from scratch. I read that this leaflet wasn't just for people like me, escaping from a restrictive lifestyle, but also for asylum seekers, refugees, people leaving foster care and also released prisoners. I realised that there could be rather a lot of people floundering in the wide space of an Outside world, and for a wide variety of reasons, varying from previous inconvenience to life threatening...

Restrictions

I sighed and wondered how we found out what I was good at if all I had done was cook and clean. I had passed a few school exams, but I didn't know what use they would be. One of the main things from my previous life had been to follow guidance from the elders and ensure that our Community did not attract attention. No transgression was permitted, drawing attention was frowned upon and would result in punishment if news reached them that anyone had been misconducting themselves. This was especially important for us girls and women. Modest dress and behaviour were essential. Always. A questioning nature had been discouraged, and so it had been difficult to find out anything. Women and girls were expected to work and serve. And be home-based. We had had to go to school, as that was the law, but I had seen other women working, in shops and even driving buses. As I had grown up, I had seen the rigidity of our world, I attended a local primary school where very many Outside children went too. There were about twelve of us from our Community, all aged between five and eight, as we would then move to our own school - a minibus came to take my older sisters and brother there every morning whereas I walked to my school with my younger brother and sister and my mother. We never took my poor sister; she was left at home in her bed until my mother returned. I saw the Outside children walking and running together, they would visit each other's houses and talk of parties. I didn't know what parties were, but they all seemed to go to them and have a lot of food. I saw a lot of things whilst I was at that school, but I didn't ask anything, as I had my sisters and other children from church there and we sometimes had sessions where we were all together without the Outside children. I realised much later that we had been withdrawn from certain topics of learning as these didn't support our Community's beliefs and restrictions. My mother always talked to us on the way to school and came to collect us at lunchtimes too. We had lunch at home, and so we missed the midday playtime. Morning playtime was good though, we met the others from our Community and climbed on the playground equipment. We didn't have such things at our own houses. It seemed that a lot of the other children seemed to be happy, although there were some that were quite fierce, and pushed and hit others. I could see why I shouldn't spend time with them, but the others, who spoke to me and tried to play with me and asked if I could go to their houses - they would ask their mothers to ask mine, what did they do that was so wrong? I had asked my mother once, and only once, why we couldn't meet with these other people. The explanation she gave was that those living in the Outside world lived wicked lives, they had no respect for God and so were all condemned to Hell, and any association by us would attract that damnation. We were told that the wickedness of the Outside world meant that the world would come to an end in a sort of battle of Armageddon. As true believers, we would be saved by God and be transported to Heaven in an exaltation of gratitude that we had supported Him for so long. Everyone from the Outside world would be going to Hell, and we would never see them again. Heaven would consist of all our forefathers; our relations and family members who had followed God so faithfully.

I never asked again because she was so very horrified by my question, which had apparently demonstrated Disobedience, Disrespect for her and Impudence and Rudeness to God, that I had been taken to the bathroom and she had washed my mouth with soap. I had been extremely sick and had been put in my bedroom. I had stayed there for a week, the sisters who also slept there had been forbidden to speak to me, and the one time I did try to speak to them I had been taken to the hallway and left to sleep there for the night. They had brought me food every evening, and I had water too; they let me go to the bathroom to use the toilet, but I had not been allowed to wash as I had spoken aloud such unclean thoughts. After a week of this punishment, I had been taken downstairs to speak to my father; he asked if there was anything I wanted to ask about what God wanted us to do. I had said No, and only then had I been allowed to return to the bathroom to wash, and finally change into clean clothes. Then we went to our regular Sunday morning church service, and I was extra careful to behave perfectly. This happened as I reached the end of my time at that school, so I would have been almost eight years old. I suppose that my mother had wanted to ensure that I never said anything similar again, as to have asked in anyone else's hearing would have brought shame on her and my father. The way that shame was dealt with was similar to the way that she had treated me, except it would have been the whole household in isolation, rebuffed by the main Community, at the order of the church, and possibly for much longer than a week. The tricky thing was that such transgressions were not necessarily set aside once the punishment had been completed. Luckily no one else had heard me ask, so she was able to carry out the punishment unhindered. We had not attended the church meetings that week as my father had been away from home visiting with other church men at one of the meetings sometimes held with the Main Authority, who was in direct communication with God, and so spoke to all of us with God's authority. This person was never questioned and was held in the highest regard by the whole church. It was an honour to be invited to a meeting with him, and the local church members would be in a state of great agitation until the house of rest was selected. This was a house where the Main Authority would choose as his resting place whilst he was away from his own home at the meeting. A household would be selected, and the man would inform his wife that she would have a number of people to accommodate on certain days. She would be expected to provide a high-quality meal for the visitors and her own family, with sleeping accommodation provided too. This could mean that the children would have to give up their own beds for the parents, as they would of course have to relinquish their own room for the visitors. If more beds were required, more than one household would be providing accommodation. This was a huge disruption to family life but was regarded as a great honour for the hosting family. Our family home had never been selected as it was known that some disgrace had caused the burden of my poor sister. Such a household would never attract an honour, as the disgrace would necessarily transfer to the visitors. Whilst many people knew of my poor sister, she was never included in any church meetings, or referred to by anyone. It was supposed that the disgrace was my mother's as she had borne such a child. It was unsurprising that there were no more babies after my poor sister. My mother was ashamed and only took her out into our back garden occasionally.

'I'm sure we can arrange something. What might be a good idea is if we find you a job that includes some training for a year or so, then you can apply for a university place and get a proper education. If we think carefully about the options, we can find you a home in a city where you can have that job and a university place.' Libby was smiling, she was positive that I would be able to stand on my own feet. The idea of this was exhausting and liberating. I was delighted that such possibilities existed. She handed me a small box. 'Here's something else, it's a mobile phone. Very basic, but it's yours, and not tracked. Being on the Outside means you can choose where you go. You are free. We can set this up so that my number is in it, and you can ring me or message me, but no one will be checking up.' This was a big thing, all the very limited technology available to Community members had been supplied to the Community from a central source, there were tracking devices on them to ensure that we were not visiting places we shouldn't, either on the Internet or physically in the town. I had never had my own mobile phone until now, so to have this one was an exciting experience. She said that we could set it up now, or later. If I wanted to add in other people's numbers we could, and we could practice using it in case I needed to use it when I was alone. I would need a bank account next, and could I drive? Did I have my national insurance number? All of this sounded a bit strange. A bank account? I definitely didn't have one of those! Of course, I couldn't drive, only men drove. If we needed to go anywhere, we walked. Or asked for a lift from our male relations. My oldest brother had his own car and as soon as my younger one gained his driving licence, he too would get a car. Typically, as soon as boys were old enough to drive, they were taught by the men. Once they passed the test, they would have a car as they would need that to get to work.

   I tore off the plastic from the box containing the phone and we set it up as the instruction booklet suggested. We added Libby in as a contact and made a note of the phone's number. Libby suggested that I learned it as most Outside people knew their mobile numbers and it would help me to fit in. We spent some time repeating the number, chanting it, and singing it. I felt a bit silly, but it was helping me to remember it. Then we practised using the phone, Libby called it, and I answered it. Then I called her, and she answered. I learned how to dismiss a call, how to call someone back and how to listen to a voicemail message. Libby was very patient with me, and I appreciated her kindness. It was just over 24 hours since I had left my old life and I was well on the way to my new one. We were surprised when the doorbell rang, and Hector paid us a visit. He came into the house and Libby offered him a cup of tea. Whilst she was in the kitchen, he asked me how I was getting on, I told him of my new clothes, hair and phone. I laughed as I recalled how Libby and I had tried to remember the number. I saw that he had his own phone in his hand, and he smiled.

'You look so beautiful when you laugh, you should laugh more. Did you get to the point when you could remember the number?'

I stopped laughing when he said that, then remembering the number, said it out loud.

'Well done,' he said. 'Say it again, to be sure it wasn't a fluke...'

I said it again, and he smiled.

'That's really great, you're doing so well!' He turned to Libby as she entered with the of mugs of tea on a blue and green tray and complimented both of us on getting so far with the change to my new life. We chatted as we drank the steaming tea and Hector spoke of others whom the network had assisted. Finally, the mugs were replaced on the tray and Hector stood up to leave. 'I'm glad it's going so well, onwards and upwards!'

'I'm really very proud of Mary,' smiled Libby, 'she has had a very busy day! But we've achieved so much, we're well on to the next stage. Paperwork next, then a job!'

Official stuff

Libby asked if I'd managed to bring any paperwork with me. I had been able to get my birth certificate from the pile that my mother kept in the kitchen. My father had the boys' certificates as they would need to register for their jobs. We girls only needed ours when we got married. She explained that I would need to register for a social security number, which would help me to get employment and learn to drive. We talked through a few ideas of work, as my main experience had been housekeeping, there were a few options - I could work in a hotel, on the housekeeping team, or in a care home, or in a residential school. Libby suggested that the school option might be the best, as I would be able to live there too, and being in an educational setting may be helpful as I probably would come across topics new to me. She explained that she had left her old life at 15, and necessarily had gone to a new school. The differences that she had discovered had been life changing for her and had encouraged her to make sure that as many children as she could come into contact with would find out the truth about the world in which they lived. She realised that her education up to that point had been severely restricted, almost censored. She said that children in Outside schools had lessons on how to live safely in relationships, that a lot of the treatment that we accepted from others in the Community was not permitted on the Outside, and that there was so much about science that was not told to us.

She had learned about different religions and sects and cults, and she saw the Community very differently now. She was inspired to help as many girls to get out as she could and had worked hard with others to put into practice this route to achieve that. The money they used to help people like me, which had paid for my new clothes and haircut, was donated by Libby herself, and others who had used the Network's assistance to leave. I resolved that, when I was settled and secure, I too would donate money for at least one person to be assisted. I could see that it wouldn't only be girls who wanted to leave, the experiences of my father and Libby's father showed that the Community wasn't a good place for many people. The younger men would be sent to different businesses as labourers, and only those who fitted the mould necessary for communicating effectively with the Outside would be promoted to business owners. If they hadn't got the right connections within the Community, they could be faced with a lifetime of employment in unregulated environments. They would be expected to obey their employers and would know that their entire future security would rely on the approval of their senior colleagues. I realised now that some of the younger men my brothers' ages were shuttled around from workplace to workplace with no great future ahead of them. The Senior Men seemed to have quite big houses, and many children. Sons were, of course, valued more than daughters as they would continue the family name and business if there was one. Daughters would be sent away to be married at some stage, and so only occasionally see their parents. It would be up to the parents to maintain any contact as the daughters' priority would be their new families.

It was amazing to hear how the Network had been set up, and that Libby had learned so much since she had left. I, too, would love to learn more and so we decided that I should look for a job in a school. As Libby worked in a school, she had links to other schools and could try to find out if there were any jobs available, the school she worked in took children on a daily basis, like the Outside school I had gone to when I was very young, and the Community school too. We had had Outside teachers in the Community school as Community people couldn't easily train as teachers, we weren't allowed to go to college or university, so we could only work in businesses set up by other Community members. I remembered that none of the teachers had lasted very long in the school's employ, they arrived and were very smiley at first, then began to get quieter and usually within a year, they had left. I know that there were a lot of mothers who helped at the school, and sometimes they sat in the classrooms. Actually, quite a lot of the time they sat in the classrooms. They didn't speak, especially if the teacher was a man. Most of our teachers were women, but not one teacher was there for as long as I had been. I was there for ten years, and the school principal was a man from our Community, but all the teachers were from the Outside. The principal would have regular weekly meetings with the Senior Men from our Community and these meetings could last for hours. Sometimes a teacher would go into the meeting, then usually leave within a day or so. We would be told that the teacher had been weak or proven to be sinful and would not be seen in school again. This was quite difficult, as many of these teachers were kind, and seemed to enjoy teaching us, to begin with anyway. By the time they went into the meetings they were coming to school looking tired and not talking as much. They brought us information on papers which they only gave to us to read if there wasn't a Classroom Mother present. Usually, a meeting would follow this, and then the teacher would leave almost immediately.

I sometimes felt sorry for the teachers, as I had seen one or two crying in their cars before they drove home. I don't think they knew how crying was seen by us as being so weak. We didn't ever cry. Once we started school, we were expected to be quiet, babies were allowed to cry, but once they learned to talk, they were left if they cried. When they stopped crying their mothers would pick them up and praise them. I hadn't cried for all my life within the Community, the tears had only come during my run from the meeting hall, through the town to meet Libby. Once the teachers were seen crying, they would leave. I liked some of them very much, but we could never talk to them. Classroom Mothers would stand up and walk towards us if we tried to talk, then a message would be sent to our mothers, and we would be in trouble when we got home. Trouble of the no tea and no talking type. The emphasis on being good, compliant and behaving well was so heavy, we girls learned at a very young age that we were not here to please ourselves, we were here to serve others, and to work. There was a room at school where we took our lunches to eat them, we were not allowed to eat with those from the Outside, so our teachers were only able to eat their lunches, brought from their own homes, after we had done so; we would sit outside in the yard where the Classroom Mothers would also be – we could play if we liked, sometimes the boys played football, and the girls hid from each other. Once the teachers had eaten their lunches and tidied up the room, a bell would ring, and we would go back into the classrooms.

My mother never came to the school, it was understood that the shame due to her burden of my poor sister would affect the other mothers, and sometimes I did see some of the mothers telling their children not to talk to me because of the shame. The children whose fathers were the readers in their meetings were always talking to other children, and I would see and hear the mothers encouraging their children to talk to or sit with these men's children. I knew that my father would never be a reader, because of my mother and my poor sister. It was a heavy burden for him, my mother's sister had sometimes spoken of the burden. He had started to speak at the meetings before my poor sister had been born but, of course, he couldn't afterwards. He had had to leave the front rows and now sat further back on the row in front of the women. My brothers sat with him too. We girls sat six rows behind them with my mother and this had been the routine since my poor sister had been born.

There was a space between us and the next family. They too were burdened; I think by the mother's behaviour. There were rumours that she had been seen arguing in the street with an Outsider, she had been with her husband in their car when he had stopped to go into a shop. They had run out of whisky, and he had gone to buy some for a lunch they were hosting at the weekend. Whilst he was in the shop, a traffic warden had stuck a label on the car and then knocked on the car window, the wife had opened the door as the keys were with her husband, and the warden had told her she couldn't park there. She had said that her husband would be back in a minute and the warden had told her to never mind that, get the car moved. She had eventually shouted at the warden, and this had been witnessed by another member of the church who had reported her dreadful behaviour to her husband who had, in turn, informed the Senior Men. She had received a punishment for such dreadful behaviour, from her husband and the church too. She had been isolated in her home for a month, her children had gone to live with another family as she had been in her bedroom, apart from getting food from the kitchen. This had started to run out, as her husband had gone to stay with one of the Senior Men to receive education as he had so obviously failed in his duty by allowing such behaviour by his wife whilst she had been out with him; by the end of the month, it was said she was eating only potatoes. The whisky had not been needed for the lunch as this privilege had been immediately withdrawn. The husband had taken it to one of the Senior Men's houses, and it had stayed there.

The wife had been collected by her husband that final Sunday morning, and he had brought her into the meeting. Her children were present, but she had not been able to see or speak to them. She had been called into the front of the congregation and asked to describe her behaviour. Other women had laughed as she had done so, and the men had glared at her. Then she was asked what she wanted to say, and she had begged for forgiveness, from God, from the church, from those present, from her husband. She had been told that consideration would take place and she had been discussed by the men as she stood to one side. She could not speak as they did so, she had stood there with her head bowed and held her hands linked behind her. One or two of the men had seen a tear fall onto the floor during their discussion and this had brought her further ridicule. Her weakness was discussed, her lack of demureness and her inability to hold her tongue. It was decided that she should resume her full duties in the home and in the church but that she should not speak at all until the next Sunday meeting. She almost collapsed with gratitude that she was allowed to return to the church, to receive her family, and she had carried out her punishment. She had not spoken to anyone for the following week, and I could now see that all this must have been exceedingly difficult for her children, three of whom were very young, and not yet at school. Whilst she had been able to cook and care for them, hug them and take the older one to school, she had not been allowed to speak. She received full forgiveness at the church meeting the following Sunday but, of course, she was now considered a burden to her husband, and he was moved to the back row of the men's section, as she was delivered to the back row of the women's. Despite the similarity of the burdens, they both being of disgrace, the families were not able to mix. As burdened families, they were tolerated. It showed that the penalties for misbehaviour were long lasting, and the fear of this treatment meant that others were incredibly careful in their actions.

It was easy to see how I had learned whilst with my family, but the thought of learning more really excited me. Libby had once had the life I had left, and she was doing really well on the Outside, so I was looking forward to seeing if I could do so too. She started to message her contacts to see if there was a space in a boarding school for a housekeeper. After a few days we heard back from one of them saying that there was a short-term position, for one term only, at a boarding school about thirty miles away. Libby was to ring if she wanted to find out more.

We looked up the school online, Libby showed me how to search on the Internet. I had heard of the Internet but hadn't ever searched. We had used computers at school, but they had been prepared by the school, so all we did was switch them on and look at the information on the screen. Sometimes we could type onto the screen through a separate keyboard, but it wasn't anything like what Libby was doing, her fingers were almost a blur as she tapped on the keyboard which was half of her computer. She told me it was a laptop, and she could carry it around in a specially made backpack; soon there were pictures of the school on the screen and people's photographs. Libby showed me the photograph of the lady she should ring for more information. She looked kind, and as if she was a little older than my mother. We decided to call her and find out what was involved. After a quick conversation, it was decided that we should go and meet with the lady, who was called Elizabeth, as my situation was quite unusual.

Interview

Driving down to the school, which was called Hornbeam Hall School, we chatted about the changes that had taken place, Libby recounted some of her own experiences since she had left, and what had happened to her sisters since their new lives had begun. Her elder sister had got married, to a man she had met on the Outside, who worked on his family's farm in the next county. As she had been earmarked for marriage at the time of leaving, she had been worried about getting married to anyone. Their father had been approached by Senior Men, from whom he had learned that that she should marry soon, as she had reached 18, and they had someone in mind for her who lived in the north of the country. He had a printing business and worked with his brothers; he was getting a house ready for her, and also, she would look after his recently widowed and ailing mother. Libby's father was overwhelmed at the thought of losing his beloved first-born, as a man with no sons he occupied the middle rows of seats in church, neither disgraced nor burdened, but obviously without the necessary qualities for leadership or progressing the church or Community. He was close to his daughters and hadn't been able to face handing one over. Knowing that was the rule was one thing, doing it was another. He had worried about this for a while, then decided that he had enough business contacts in the Outside to ensure that he could make enough of a living to support them all, as his business and house would be taken by the church if he wasn't there. Knowing this, he had taken all their personal paperwork, birth certificates and the documents for his car; told all three daughters to pack some clothes into one small bag each and, quietly, they all five got into the car and drove away. He drove to an address of a business contact on the Outside and asked him for assistance. The man had booked them into a hotel for a week, and met with him daily, offering guidance on what to do next. As they would be sought, he had left behind nothing that would enable them to be found. He had destroyed all his personal papers other than those taken with him, he had dropped his mobile phone into the lavatory, thus effectively destroying it and not allowing any tracking device to take effect. By only taking one bag each, they had not drawn any attention to their departure, and by driving away at night they had ensured that no one would have noticed. Their supporter had been so very kind, as it had been a huge risk taken by the family, without his help they may have had to return, which would have been an overwhelming situation for them. The Outsider had been kind and had helped more than they had dared to hope. He had found them a place to live and even employed the father to allow him the dignity of supporting his family. As the years had gone by, Libby's father had established himself well business-wise, had managed to support his family, and encouraged his wife in her dream of having a part-time job of her own. She worked each morning in a shop, and her employer was understanding and allowed her to prioritise her children if they were unwell. They hardly ever were, and it was a good life that they had had. Libby's family grew to enjoy their new home, and way of life. All these years later, all three daughters were now working and two of them had completed study at university. The youngest was still undertaking her studies, it had taken her a bit longer due to illness.

Our chat had taken up the entire journey, and before long we had arrived at Hornbeam Hall School. There were dozens of big trees, which Libby said could be hornbeams, forming an avenue either side of the long driveway leading from the public road, over some lovely open green space. We drove up to a huge building, like a palace, and stopped outside the front door. It was the Easter holidays, as Libby had mentioned on my arrival at her house, and so not many people were about. I could see some a way off behind some wire fencing, and a few were walking under the trees. I couldn't see any children although there were a few dogs. As we got out of the car, the lady whose photo we had seen on the screen came down the steps to meet us. 'Hello! You must be Libby and Mary.'

We followed her into a little room with a table and chairs in, and lots of green plants and books on shelves. Libby explained that I was looking for a job with accommodation and was experienced in housekeeping. Elizabeth spoke of the position that was available here, and this meeting was to see if I was a good fit. Libby stated that this would be my first job, and that I had grown up in a very protected environment. My life experiences were few, but I knew how to do the work that was needed, and I would like to learn about meeting people. Elizabeth listened and said that I wouldn't necessarily need to come into contact with the pupils, but did I have clearance to work with children? Libby explained that due to family circumstances I didn't yet have my social security number, but this was being processed. Elizabeth thought that we could work with that and suggested that we all go along to meet with the Head.

Libby caught my eye, 'That would be the Head Teacher, I suppose, or Principal.'

'Yes, that's right. Our current Head is Mrs Higgins. She's very experienced and has worked here for about twelve years. She's probably playing tennis.'

We followed Elizabeth along corridors, the walls of which were covered in displays of work done by the pupils in the school. Some of the walls had shelf units which contained models made by the children, others contained huge silver cups and medals, individually inscribed. It looked as if this school was much bigger and more active than the ones I had attended. We left the building through a different door and followed Elizabeth to the wire fencing behind which some people were running about hitting a ball with big paddles - this must be tennis!

A tall woman approached, holding one of the paddles, which I could now see had a sort of mesh stretched tightly across the open circle at one end of the paddle which had been hitting a small bright yellow ball between the people, Elizabeth was holding the other end which had looked like a coloured stalk.

'Hello, you must be Libby and Mary! Shall we sit over here?' She smiled and led the way to a table with benches either side, beneath a huge old oak tree. It must have been hundreds of years old and was like one in the grounds of the school I had attended. We had hidden behind it during our games after lunch sometimes, and I remembered the feel of the ridges in the bark, and the big root at the side of the tree, where it had worn smooth under the hands and feet of countless children over the years. The building had been used as a village school for over a hundred years; our Community had bought it about ten years prior to my attendance there, intending as a site for our church meetings but the local people had objected to our plans to either knock it (and the trees) down and build a meeting hall, or to convert it to a meeting room, so it had been decided to use it as a school, and children arrived from all over the county every morning. The local people had complained about that as the traffic involved caused delays, but the council had allowed it to progress.

I looked across the table at Mrs Higgins, she smiled and asked what I thought about working in a school. I explained that I was looking forward to learning and liked the atmosphere of the school. She smiled again and started to talk about the work that would be needed, and the reason for the short notice. One of the housekeepers had had to attend a family emergency so had decided to stay with their family member for a few weeks. The work was needed for the school term ahead only, as it was likely that the situation would be resolved before the Autumn term. If I was to take on the job, I would need to live at the school, and work a split shift. This sounded confusing, and so did more of what was said. I would get paid to my bank account and be on full board. I would need to provide my social security number and fill in an application form. A security check would be done and, until the results came through, I would not be able to be in the same place as the pupils; this wasn't likely to hinder my work as I would work from 7am to 10am, then 2pm to 6pm. This would be my routine for each weekday as there was a weekend team. Full board meant I would get three meals every day, regardless of whether it was my working day or not. I would get weekends off but could remain at the school if I wanted to, I could use the learning facilities, or play sports with any other resident staff, when the facilities were closed to the pupils. This tended to be during the later parts of the evenings, although the swimming pool was open for staff use every morning between 6am and 7.30am. It all sounded very exciting, and I think Mrs Higgins could sense my enthusiasm, as she smiled again and asked Elizabeth to show me around the school, and where I would be staying. We walked up stairs and along corridors, down steps and through halls. I knew I wouldn't find my way around alone straightaway, but as soon as I saw the room I would be living in if I got the job here, I was certain that I could manage the work, I could expand my education and enjoy the atmosphere here. When we got back to the tennis area I nodded to Libby.

'This would work for you, I think, Mary. What can we do now, Mrs Higgins?'

'If you would like the post, Mary, we can work something out. We need you to be here by the end of the week, and if you can fill the forms in today, we can process the formalities.'

Libby and I were taken back to the first room, it was Elizabeth's office apparently, I liked the idea of having an office. It seemed to be just for her, she had her own computer and telephone and lots of information stuck to the walls. We wrote all my information onto the forms and answered as many questions as we could, my limited experience was the main issue, but I did the best I could. Having left the papers with Elizabeth and received written information about my job, we drove back to Libby's house. When we opened the door, and Libby had disabled the alarm - I was getting used to the amount of bleeping that took place in houses on the Outside - I could see that the blue light was flashing again. It seemed that another message had been left, so I left Libby pressing buttons whilst I went to make some tea. I could hear the electronic voice again, then another human voice spoke, the words were a bit muffled as the kettle boiled and I rustled biscuit packets. Then I heard another voice, and I could hear the higher pitch of Sarah's voice saying 'Libby, we need to chat, let me know when you're back, I need to come round.'

We drank our tea, and Libby said that the first voice had been the police, they wanted to talk to us again, she was going to ring them back, and hoped to arrange a meeting before the end of the week. We weren't sure why they would want to come back to us so soon, so decided that we would see what was asked. We arranged to see them the following day, they would call in during the afternoon. Then Sarah arranged to come round within the hour. It had been a good day so far, I just needed to get what I needed ready for my transfer to school. I would be given an overall, but I would need to wear my own clothes underneath. I didn't want to wear my dress, it was a reminder of bad things, it could stay behind. All my possessions and clothes would fit into those big bags we had got during the shopping trip. My shoulder bag would contain my new scarf and other items that I had been given by Libby, it wouldn't take long for me to pack, or unpack at the other end. By now I could hear that Sarah had arrived. I could hear them talking and ran downstairs to chat with them. As I entered the room, they stopped talking and asked me if I would like another cup of tea, I volunteered to be tea-maker and I could hear them talking quietly as I prepared our drinks. When I went back in with the tray, they asked me to sit down and started to talk about Hector.

New start

We talked until it got dark, there were so many questions! Hector had been in conversation with more than one group trying to help others, apparently, and had been arranging for some of the people involved to work in a hotel. There seemed to be some confusion about who had gone to which hotel, and Sarah had decided to ask what my plans were, and she and Libby had been chatting about how they could ensure the best way of arranging things for others using the network. Libby had explained how I had found the role at the school, and it hadn't included Hector. There were other people involved in the rescue group; it seemed to involve quite a few people in the arrangements. There was a group of hosts - people like Libby who received people like me, who would allow us to stay for a few days whilst we changed our appearance and arranged our new jobs. I hadn't thought that there may be several of us trying to make new lives, when I had seen the message from the group, with a phone number to ring. I had seen a card stuck to the window as I went into the clothing shop where I shopped for my dresses. 'Are you living the life you want? Do you need help to leave the life you have? We can help you. Ring us when it is safe to do so.' The lady behind the counter had seen me looking at the note in the window, and had spoken to me as I went in. She had asked if I wanted to borrow a pencil and paper. I had been so startled, I couldn't think of anything to say, but she had put them down in front of me, saying that no one was around. I wrote down the number and pushed the paper down under my clothing, inside my vest. I gave back the notebook and pencil, smiling briefly at the lady. She smiled back and whispered, 'Good Luck, we're here if you need us.'

I had kept that slip of paper inside my vest for the rest of the day. I felt as if there was a bomb ticking inside my chest. I was so apprehensive; I was sure that my mother and my sisters could see that there was something different and I tried so hard to be my usual self. I could see my mother looking carefully at me, and I carried on with my chores, it was laundry day, and I had returned from the shops to bring in the washing and start the ironing. It would take until we left for church to get the laundry folded, ironed and put away. As I ironed, I thought and thought about the shop lady, her kindness and the phone number. What should I do? The thought of marrying soon was scary, I was close to being 20, and women did need to be married by then. My father had been asked to a meeting with the Senior Men in a few days' time and this could only mean that it was to discuss my marriage. My older sister had been told of her marriage; it had been to a man from a town over a hundred miles away. She had left to marry him, to work in his business and then to have his children. After a few weeks of marriage, he had been killed in a car accident and she had returned to us until a replacement could be found. I think it was going to take some time until she was promised to another man as, having been married, she was not an ideal first wife. If a man whose wife had died was found, she would be married to him. She had not had her husband's baby, so it wasn't certain if she could become a mother. It was likely that she would go to a man who had motherless children, and she would probably have some of her own children too. Families tended to have several children, girls were encouraged to think of themselves as mothers-in-waiting, almost. I think I had not followed that thought due to a teacher I had once had at school. I had been aged about twelve, and we had been learning from a young lady teacher about geography. The teacher had described the action of glaciers and water erosion in the mountainous regions, and I had asked a question about the strata she had mentioned. The Classroom

Mother had not yet returned from taking a boy to the sickroom as he had claimed to feel unwell. Boys were precious, so he was attended to straightaway. Other children in the room were drawing a sketch of the layers of rocks, following the description of the formation of different layers of rocks due to changes in sediment but I must have looked puzzled because she asked me to come to her desk. I walked up to it as she rummaged in her bag. She had brought out her mobile phone and started to show me photographs of striped rocks. She explained that she had been out for a walk on the previous Sunday and had taken some photographs. She showed me how to slide my finger across the screen to move to the next photograph, and how I could use two fingers to make a part of the photograph bigger. I looked at several pictures showing the rocks, the layers were quite clear, and seemed to stand out from the land behind, she explained that this was because they were made of a harder rock, which would have washed down the ancient riverbed by a long-gone river. Then the next photograph was of my teacher. She was smiling at the camera, and had a small black, brown and white dog held against her chest; leaning against her was a man, his face was against the side of her face, and he was kissing her cheek. I could see that he had an arm around her, and his other hand was in front of all three of them, in a thumbs-up pose. I looked up at the teacher and she saw the photo I was looking at.

'Oh,' she said, 'that's a selfie I took of me with Toby, my boyfriend, he had just proposed, and I had said Yes, so he's celebrating. I think he was quite relieved; he must have been rather nervous. We were at the top of the hill, and it was really hot, so I'd been carrying Tinker, who was panting rather a lot! We were quite glad to get home, Sunday was really quite a scorcher, wasn't it?' She held her left hand out to me with the fingers widespread, 'he forgot to take the ring with him, he gave it to me when we got home, he had hidden it in his sock drawer!' On her third finger was a slim silver ring with a beautiful pale blue glittering stone in it. She looked at it and smiled, 'I'm really very lucky, we've been living together for over a year, so it's time we started to think about getting married, we're going to tell our parents at the weekend...'

This pronouncement had so many thoughts whirling around inside my head - she had gone out on a Sunday; with a man who wasn't her husband; she was holding a dog, which appeared to be her pet; she was wearing a top which showed her arms, and the top part of her chest; she had a man living in her house who wasn't her brother; she was going to marry a man and her parents didn't know; she was allowing a man to kiss her, in public; and also, she regarded herself as very lucky. This was the most surprise to me - all those dangerous and forbidden things were happening to her, and she felt lucky! I looked at her in silence, but her happiness had reached me, and I smiled at her. The look I saw in her eyes was the same as when I saw my mother at church, when the prayers were being said. It was the only time I saw her look like this, the only time she smiled so peacefully. At all other times she had a worried, strained, tired look to her face, but her expression during prayers was the same look as my teacher as she talked of her boyfriend and her dog. This was a huge puzzle; how could such dreadful things make someone so lovely so happy? This was the first time that I had the feeling that maybe there were other ways to live. I had thought of that time in school many times since, my teacher was such a lovely, kind lady who so clearly enjoyed teaching us children. She certainly didn't seem to be suffering from the wickedness of the world, and I had had many thoughts about what she had said, particularly because I had seen the look in her eyes. The other children had started to nudge each other, and whisper, so she had stood up and brought everyone's attention to the big board on the wall and she had started to draw a riverbed, describing the way in which erosion took place. The children had stopped whispering, although one of the boys had looked at me rather than at the board. The Classroom Mother had returned during the river description, and the boy had asked to speak to her after the lesson. The lovely teacher had not returned to school the following day, she had not been given the chance to cry in her car, she had been summoned to the principal's room and later she had been walked to her car and she had driven off. An announcement had been made saying that she had misled the school about her suitability for teaching and a new teacher had arrived a week or so later. I had received isolation punishment for a week at school, for looking at the photograph and listening to immoral language. Boyfriends were not part of our society, much less discussions about living with one. I should have reported her immediately the Classroom Mother returned, not allowed the boy to witness my moral failure on the count of listening, and then not reporting. I was not allowed to talk to anyone at school for the week following, and the enforced isolation allowed me to reflect on the photographs. I didn't forget the look in her eyes, and I wished so much that I could talk to her again.

  I looked at my mother as I finished the ironing and lifted the pile of crisply folded shirts and linen to carry it upstairs. The paper rustled quietly in my clothes as I leaned forward, and after I had returned the ironed clothes to their dark closets and drawers, I went into the bathroom. Locking the door, I felt for the paper and read the numbers written on it. There were eleven numbers, how could I remember these? I needed a pen! There were no pens to hand, so I quickly collected one from the hallway and returned to the sanctuary of the bathroom. Sharing bedrooms as we did, I knew that I would not be able to look at the paper without anyone seeing me do so. I crouched on the bathroom floor, pushed down my left sock and, twisting my leg, I copied the number from the paper onto the inside of my ankle, on the bone. I checked that the numbers were correct and crumpled up the paper into a small ball. I threw it into the toilet bowl and then turned my attention to my right ankle. I rubbed hard at the skin above the outside of the ankle bone with the lid of the pen. Gritting my teeth, I rubbed and rubbed until the skin was raw and eventually blood showed. Pulling up my socks I leaned to the lavatory and hauled the handle dangling from the cistern near the ceiling. The water frothed in the bowl and then gradually settled, the pipes rattled slightly, and the tank gulped further supplies into its elevated position. I ran the basin taps and adjusted the towel on the rail slightly, as if I had indeed been in the bathroom for natural purposes, rather than to record my escape route.

  I returned to the kitchen and asked my mother if I could please have a sticking plaster? I had caught my ankle on a stone step and wanted to protect the graze as it healed. Mother looked at me and insisted on seeing the wound, I showed her, and she gave me a long look. Yes, she said, you may. Handing me the first aid kit, she watched as I took a band aid and held it beside my scratched leg, ensuring that the dressing was large enough to cover the oozing blood. Just then my older sister arrived with a big box of vegetables and managed to drop a few potatoes as she thudded the harvest down onto the shabby wooden table. Taking advantage of my mother's efforts to recapture the errant items I swiftly took an extra sticking plaster and slid it inside my sock. I would cover the number with this as soon as I could. As they turned to me a moment later, I was peeling off the paper and affixing the plaster to my raw graze. I dropped the wrapper into the bin and resumed my household duties. Peeling the reluctant potatoes and adding the pieces to a large pan, we prepared the evening meal. This would slowly cook whilst we attended church, and we could then eat on our return, a couple of hours later.

Sitting in the back row at church, I allowed my mind to drift over the possibility of making a change. My glance crept around to her face, and I could see the expression which I had seen in my teacher's eyes all those years earlier. The elder was speaking about the sustenance of God, how we would all live for eternity in heaven if we followed his teachings. Mother gazed into the centre of the room, seeing the man standing, holding the microphone and slowly turning to address the men sitting in the front row. The hall had the shape reminiscent of an amphitheatre and those speaking would stand at the bottom of twin embankments of seats. The men listened and watched the speaker. He made eye contact with each of the front row, which defined them as seniors, or elders. Those holding less significance in the Community sat behind and, even further back, we women and children could hear every word, thanks to the microphone system, but were less able to make eye contact. In fact, it was discouraged, as it wasn't demure behaviour - looking a man in the eye, the very idea! Mother was looking towards the speaker, but I felt that her focus was far, far away. Her eyes were unfocused, and she sat still. As still as a statue that I had seen in one of our school geography books. It had been of a woman, gazing downwards slightly, as she sat on a rock beside the sea. Her legs had blended together as she sat, lost in her own thoughts, with her hands folded together in her lap, exactly as my mother was seated now. I wondered what her thoughts were, and how they managed to consume her in the way she seemed to be so completely overtaken. Suddenly there was a shrill whine, as the speaker handed the microphone to another man, also from the front row. Mother's shoulders jerked slightly, and she resumed her focus back in the room as the speakers changed places.

The second man began to talk, 'Brothers, we must address the following situation that could arise should the ...' His voice continued rather monotonously, and I resumed my thoughts of an alternative life. After church there were always a few minutes when families exchanged words of support, criticism or fellowship, depending on whether there were any active situations under scrutiny at that time. People tended to mix, without remaining in their family groups, and this could be a time when I could make my break. My family was seated on the back row, and there was a door beside my end of row chair. This allowed those on the back rows to leave the room without disturbing the lower rows of seniors. Occasionally a small child or a baby would need attention and the mother would leave the room during the meeting, this was ordinarily frowned upon, despised by the men, but the noise made by a hungry baby was too distracting, even if it was disturbing only the women. I thought that I could possibly leave the room first and then the building. The younger men who acted as gatekeepers would have left their posts by the time the meeting was ending, as they would have locked the main doors after the meeting began and entered the main hall themselves. I would be able to run down the stairs, having whispered to my mother my need for the toilet, and make my escape through the fire door beside these facilities. I wouldn't dare to open the main doors, the draught from them would alert too many to a change in routine, as the gatekeepers would usually unlock them as the hall cleared and the foyer filled with quiet conversation. I was sure that I could make my escape in these few minutes. All I had to do was decide when it would be and make a call to the number under the band aid on my left ankle.

Calling for help

It took some time for me to see how the phone call could be made; I knew that I would have to make the call from the house telephone, when everyone was out. This happened so rarely. Usually, my mother was in the house, my poor sister was always there although she was of no consequence in my plans, and at least one of my older brother and sisters was usually there.

I waited and waited. More than once I approached the silent telephone, ready to start dialling in the soundless house, only to hear footsteps in the driveway, the thud of a closing car door, or the rattle of a key suddenly in a lock. This was enough to drive me to another room in a single leap, and to hastily start a minor housework task which would give credibility to my presence. Eventually, an opportunity arose. My younger brother and blonde sister were both at school, my father at work and, due to sudden and crippling toothache my eldest sister had been taken to a dentist by my older brother. My older sister, with her marriage very close, had been collected by two of the wives of the Senior Men and taken to one of their homes, for guidance on her forthcoming marriage. She would be married by the end of the month and living miles away from our current home. My father had been approached by the elders about my own marriage, recently hearing that I was likely to be taken to meet my future husband shortly after my sister's wedding. This would take place in a meeting room in the town where her new home would be, with an official from the Outside to legalise the marriage. There was always an effort to keep the wedding room smart, to elicit as little comment from the Outsider as possible. It was always the woman who moved to her husband's town. He would have a business, and a home. The wife's role was to maintain the home, whilst the husband developed the business and earned the money. Choices were very limited in our world, so much of our life was dictated by the Senior Men, and our personal choices really came down to which underclothing we wanted to wear. They were all remarkably similar, but we could choose which ones. Our food choices were made by our mother, our studies by the principal and our occupation outside school was dictated by our parents whilst we were at home, we girls had chores to do, and the boys had to learn business skills, studying the methods of building a business, learning how to operate within the workplace. Then when we were at the church meetings, we had no choices to make. We knew we had to sit quietly. Making choices had not been part of our learning, not until I had seen that look in my teacher's eyes as she spoke of her life. Her gentleness had shown me that Outsiders could be good people.

As there were only three people in the house, my poor sister, my mother and I, it was likely that I may be sent to collect the surplus early new potatoes from my mother's sister's house a short walk away. She had a smaller family than my mother did, only three children, so often had spare garden produce during the relevant harvesting seasons. New potatoes were rather a treat, and I knew that my mother wouldn't want to miss this delicacy. I decided to plead sickness, so I would be left behind. My mother agreed to collect the potatoes herself, and I ran to the bathroom as if I was nauseated as she reached for her coat. I retched and coughed to add realism as my mother left. Hearing the door slam behind her, I saw her walking quickly down the front path to the street, then turned towards my aunt's house. I knew that she would be no more than ten minutes, so I pulled the band aid off my ankle and ran downstairs. Lifting the telephone receiver, I dialled the numbers as they were written on my skin. Some of them had faded a bit, where the adhesive had lifted the ink, despite my careful application of the strip, but eventually I reached the final number, and I listened impatiently as the clicking sounded the register of the number. Then a ringing sounded, my heart beat faster, as I listened, my mouth felt dry and I swallowed nervously - I watched the driveway all the time, for signs of my family returning.

A lady's voice answered, 'Hello?'

'Um. Hello, um, I got this number from the clothes shop...'

'I see. Are you wanting to make a new life?'

I paused, was I? Did I really want to go? I knew I wouldn't be able to come back, this was a huge decision. Huge. I took a deep breath, 'Yes, yes please.'

'Are you sure? Are you ready now?'

'Yes. I am.'

'There can be a car to collect you from the main car park in town one evening. What time can you get away?'

'I can come after church, tomorrow it finishes about eight o'clock.' The church Senior Men usually arranged for the meetings to start at seven o'clock, but tomorrow there was to be a visit made to a church elder who was seriously ill in hospital. They were visiting him to arrange for paperwork to be signed and had to do so during hospital visiting hours. This meant that the meeting would start much earlier than usual, at six o'clock. As soon as the children arrived home from school, they would change their clothes and we would all go straight to the meeting.

'Tomorrow? Look for a lady in a red beret. That will be me. I will wait until nine o'clock, if you need to ring again, you can use this number. See you tomorrow.'

'OK. See you tomorrow.'

I replaced the receiver and ran back to the kitchen. I'd done it. I'd arranged to leave.

...

The bright yellow and black jacket loomed through the window of the front door again that evening. PC Singh arrived shortly after the stipulated time of 5.45pm but Libby didn't appear to mind. The point of this second visit was to say that they had reviewed the CCTV from the car park and the shop through which I had run and had decided that I had indeed approached the car of my own accord, and that I had not been kidnapped. I felt the curious gaze of PC Singh as he relayed this information, he enquired of Libby how she knew Hector and she told of how the two of them had met at university as friends and, coincidentally, had settled in the same district after they had completed their studies. I felt that I may not have heard the last from the police. There was a look in PC Singh's expression that puzzled me. As if he was not saying something but wanted to ask me more questions. I didn't think about him for long though, as I had heard yet more language that I didn't understand. Libby had said after they 'had graduated' and I wanted to find out more about that. I asked her what that had meant once PC Singh had left. She had explained about the celebration at the end of her university degree course and shown me some photographs as well as her degree certificate. It looked wonderful to see such celebrations going on, the photographs she showed me included her parents. Their pride in their daughter was beautiful to see, and all three were smiling at the camera. Libby stood between her parents; she was dressed in a long black gown which reminded me of the time I had had my hair cut. On her head was a black, flat-topped hat with a sort of fringe on one side. She explained that it was a cap and gown, the cap was also known as a mortar board, and the fringe was a tassel. It was formal university dress, historically university students had worn that sort of outfit for studying, but it was now reserved for official functions only. I was so pleased that she had been successful, and I secretly resolved to achieve my own university degree, with a graduation ceremony. My eyes filled with tears though, would my mother and father attend? Could they ever be proud of me? My recent actions meant that it was a likely impossibility.

Part 2   A Fresh Start

Working woman

I looked in the mirror. Pulling my shoulder length hair into a ponytail (I had learned how to do this very quickly and had a collection of colourful scrunchies to make the process easier) I then applied a thin screen of moisturiser and a minimum of pink lipstick. Picking up my fob, which I still thought of as my magic key, I left my room, hearing the door close firmly behind me. I ran down the stairs at the end of the corridor, down to the next landing, then the next, then finally the ground floor double doors were in front of me, and I held my fob against the magnetic locking system before another loud click allowed me to push my way through to the refectory. I had thought of this as a dining room, which it was, but at Hornbeam Hall it was referred to as the refectory. I approached the counter and was greeted by the lady standing behind.

'Morning Mary! Will it be an omelette this morning or a continental plate?'

I was hungry after my hours of cleaning. I had been dusting, polishing and sweeping for two hours, and had tidied myself up ahead of the mealtime. I hesitated, the omelettes were lovely, but I was extra hungry. 'How about a bit of both?'

I nodded and Delma lifted a platter containing salami and ham, cheese and slices of different breads arranged in an attractive fan shape, and from the chilled shelves, moving to the where an omelette plate stood under the heat lamps. She slid the contents of the platter onto the plate beside the omelette and passed the warm and now very full plate to me. I placed it onto my tray, thanking her and exchanging pleasantries about the day ahead, and the weather. I knew this to be small talk, and it seemed to be essential to all interactions. Silence seemed to be unwelcome, and I had heard others refer to silences as

'Awkward'. Then, taking a small cafetière jug of fresh coffee, a mug and a tiny jug of milk, I carried my tray past the rows of white-topped tables where the pupils would sit on their arrival from the boarding houses, they would be here any moment, I was sure, and I walked quickly over to the blue-topped tables at the back of the room. I joined other staff members already seated and began to eat.

More staff were following my route, selecting their food and drinks to fuel themselves ahead of the day of teaching and learning ahead of them. They professed to learn as much as their pupils, there was never to be a state of 'knowing it all'. I was looking forward to spending time in the school library today, I was gradually reading my way through the many reference books there. I was finding out so much, about evolution, about Space, and about genetics. I had been at the school for two weeks now, cleaning the science laboratories every morning and evening, and the staff had been so passionate about their subjects I couldn't help but become involved in learning more. I had been dusting the windowsills, cleaning the shelves and wiping over the wall displays and seen many plants, posters and containers of liquids that seemed to be alive that the staff had been only too happy to share their knowledge, and had referred me to certain areas of the library shelves. I had a dictionary that accompanied my seat there, as many of the words I came across were new to me. I was extremely interested to read of so many subjects, but sad that my Community had seen fit to deprive me of so much learning. I hadn't told anyone about my background, Libby had said that it would be best to carry on as Mary, and the background we had suggested of family absence due to parental employment choices resulting in me earning some money in a series of casual jobs before leaving for university was not too far from the truth. Libby had said that staying secretive would only inspire some of the more curious staff members to probe for more information, so it would be best to allow Mrs Higgins and Elizabeth to be the only ones who could know the full story.

We had rehearsed several responses to likely questions, as it was only natural that some would be asked, I would say that I expected to see my family in the summer, and that my father worked as a civil servant carrying out research. I was to roll my eyes slightly as I said this, to try to convey the dullness of such an occupation, and to mention their personal interest in gardening too. It was best if I didn't refer to siblings, but to mention older cousins as contemporaneous relatives. I needn't actually tell any lies, as this was too much for me to do. But I could omit the truth. I could refer to hoping to study geography at university, and to mention some of the big cities that contained several universities - Birmingham and Manchester would be my suggestion, but also to say I was waiting to hear from them. I felt prepared and looked forward to going to study at a university, although studying geography wouldn't be my preference. As time went on, I was becoming more and more interested in biology. The biology of plants, people and animals was a field that I hadn't ever heard of either. We had been taught the very basics of anatomy, but I couldn't describe much more than limbs and major organs.

The books I was reading were describing how the heart worked, how the brain worked, and I had found out how babies were made and then born. This was also something I hadn't learned before and would have been what my sister was finding out about in the days before I left. Her talks with the Senior Men's wives would have been about how to conduct herself as a wife, and it was likely that such information would be communicated at that stage. I could see from the books that babies would be conceived at certain times, which could be why my oldest sister had failed to become pregnant. It was unlikely that either she or her husband had known such details, and this could explain why she hadn't gained a baby. The Community would refer to a baby as a gift from God, bestowed to those who deserved such gifts. A baby that hadn't been born with a usual appearance, as was the case with my poor sister, was seen as a punishment, a disgrace. Reading these books, I could see that this was not the reality. My mother, as the bearer of a child such as my poor sister should have been offered support, sympathy and kindness as science suggested that these things could happen because of genetics. This was a huge area of fascination to me. It seemed to me now, with the benefit of Outsider's knowledge, likely that had she had the contact with and input from the health system and their doctors that she should have had, my poor sister would have been able to have had operations and other specialist care which may have allowed her to have had a much more rewarding life, she may have been able to walk, talk and even contribute to our household in ways similar to her sisters. I was conflicted by how the Community may have failed both my poor sister and my mother. Ridiculing the two of them, limiting them so greatly within the Community in the way that they had been was, it began to appear to me, very, very cruel.

Conversation at the breakfast table continued in a desultory fashion; I had learned, during my time in the Community, how not to draw attention to myself, so I became a good listener. Being a good listener seemed to be an excellent way of learning. I learned much about my colleagues, as they became quite unguarded at times - there was a lot I didn't need to know, so I tried to forget much of the more personal knowledge I gained. Most of the staff members seemed to be single people. Some appeared to have been previously married, and were now alone for a variety of reasons, although some were married to other staff members. This seemed to be both a good thing and a bad thing. Depending on the way the teaching and learning was going, it certainly gave me some perspective on relationships. Living in the Community, I had never had friends. The other Community members were regarded as acquaintances since to regard one member as preferential to another was not acceptable. We were allowed to socialise, but we had to treat everyone the same. Some of the men and older boys there had made me feel uncomfortable, but I'd never known why. I had mentioned my feelings to my mother once, and she had said, quite sharply, that I shouldn't say things like that, that our Community wouldn't tolerate such comments that I should be a good girl, and I must be polite to everyone, as God wished. I had noticed, though, that some of the other girls looked uncomfortable when they were near those same people that had caused me uneasiness, and that they looked relieved when they could move away. At this school there was one man who made me feel uneasy and I made sure I didn't ever sit beside him at mealtimes. Today I was sitting beside one of the younger PE teachers, and he was telling me about the forthcoming Sports Day. I'd never heard of this, so I let him talk, making a note to include it in my next chat with Elizabeth. If I asked questions, I exposed my lack of understanding, and that could cause unwanted curiosity. It sounded exciting though, apparently it was on the last day of term. The pupils' parents attended a competition where the pupils would race against each other, see who could throw and jump the furthest or highest in the morning, followed by a picnic lunch, and afterwards there would be speeches and awards. Then the pupils returned home for the summer holidays, and there would be a major cleaning task to undertake! It sounded great fun - I was beginning to enjoy having fun. This, too, had been limited to reading religious books and tracts from the Great Leader, which were distributed to us by the Main Authority as he made his progress around the country. The

Great Leader lived in a different country, and rarely visited the Communities living around the world, each country had a sort of deputy, called a Main Authority to whom the Senior Men all deferred. Of course, when the Great Leader did travel abroad, the excitement was huge, and the welcome he was given was remarkable. I had not experienced such an event, but my father had done so as a young man and spoke of the occasion with such reverence that the significance of the occasion was felt by us all, even decades later. I did remember that sometimes we had played on a climbing frame in a garden when we had been included in a big lunch. This had happened before it had become apparent that my poor sister had been born in the way that she was, it had not been immediately apparent, all that was noticed that was she didn't feed as quickly as other babies and hadn't moved around as others did. We were no longer welcome after that was discovered as we were said to be cursed, and no one wanted to be cursed by association with us. To realise that I could have been learning about so many wonderful things, doing so much exercise and sport, knowing so many nice people and living in a world that was not terrifying, full of evil activities and people as I had been told since I was a small child, was upsetting. The level of the deception was becoming apparent. I began to see that I had been controlled by fear, by my parents and by my Community. I couldn't blame my parents; they had been controlled too.

Independence

Making decisions for myself had been a new challenge to be met. Libby had helped, she had accompanied me on another shopping trip before I had left for this job, and had encouraged me to choose leggings, tops and a dress, all in colours I liked. She had shown me photographs of fashionable outfits, explaining that this was also an option, but I didn't want to tie myself to any unnecessary rules, even those of my choosing. I selected clothes that I liked, that fitted me, and that I could easily wash and dry.

One thing that I had bought with some mixed feelings was a swimsuit. This appeared to be a bit bigger than my underwear joined to a bralette and made of stretchy fabric. I liked it, it felt good to be unrestricted, and I felt as if I was decent too. I was showing the full length of my legs and Libby had suggested that it was time to shave my legs! This had involved using the packet of plastic sticks that had been in my welcome pack when I had first arrived at Libby's house. They had turned out to be disposable razors - different from the huge, wooden handled blades that stood in large glass containers in our bathroom at home. One for my father and one for each of my brothers. The blades were sharpened weekly on a whet stone. Being in my family home seemed so very long ago now but was actually just over a month. Libby had shown me how to shave my legs without cutting the skin, I remembered seeing scratches on my brothers' faces as they had begun shaving. The Community men were not permitted to have any facial hair, so they had shaved each morning. Libby had suggested I shave my armpits too, and if my arms were hairy, I could shave them if I wanted to. Libby explained that it was about hygiene and social normality, women who allowed their legs to remain hairy whilst wearing shorts or swimsuits were considered unusual, although it was everyone's personal choice how they presented themselves; again, a huge difference to the rules of the Community. Such sensitive topics had never been discussed in the Community - only the skin of our hands and faces was visible and, apart from some of the elderly ladies, facial hair had not been an issue. Some of these incredibly old women appeared to have wispy moustaches, and wiry hairs randomly growing on their chins. These too attracted ridicule from the other Community members, small boys had been heard to mock this and mothers hadn't always corrected them.

Women tended not to be mentioned if they abided by the fairly strict rules of modest dress and quiet behaviour. Elderly ladies seemed to be experts at both those rules, although one or two did become rather unpredictable in their speech or behaviour. This was attributed to be a punishment from God due to past, probably secret, misdemeanours and they were swiftly excluded from meetings. They would live out the rest of their lives in the homes of their adult children, unless their needs exceeded what could be provided by their daughters or daughters-in-law and they went to live in residential care. This was costly, but there was an element of finance-sharing amongst the Community members, and it was possible, although not certain, to receive support from a central fund. This was a significant help to many but, like most support offered by the Community, could be withdrawn at any stage, without notice and without a reason. For so many, living in the Community must have been like living on a cliff edge. A cliff edge that could, at any stage, crumble and not necessarily have a ledge a few feet down to offer rescue. I remembered another family of seven people who had suddenly stopped coming to the meetings. It was a long time ago, before my poor sister had been born and before I had moved to the Community's school. I wondered what had happened to them. They had been a family of three children and their parents, and the two widowed grandmothers. The two grandmothers had been looking after their grandchildren for some time and this had given them a valued place in the family. As they had got older and the children had got bigger, they had become less able to fulfil the needs of healthy growing children, there had been occasions when one of the children had been left behind at their primary school after the other children had been collected by one of the grandmothers. Eventually a social worker had been sent by the school to the house to investigate whether the children were being cared for properly. This was considered wrong by the Community for many reasons - it demonstrated bad parenting, bad family management and attracted unwanted attention of the worst kind - critical attention - to the Community. The family had immediately been sent to the back row of the meetings which were held almost daily; and because the social workers progressed their investigation over several months the family's isolation increased. At no time were they able to explain to the Community what had happened, and the grandmother's forgetfulness would not be tolerated as a reasonable excuse for such intrusion into the ways of the Community. The Community aimed to exploit the Outside for as much gain as they could, as personal and Community wealth was very highly regarded - whilst members abided by the law to remain inconspicuous, truly little respect for the Outsiders was held by the Community. Decisions made during meetings took the place of Outside legal process - children would be moved from one family to another, marriages arranged, members could be banished or instructed to return, businesses were gained and lost, property was moved from one person to another all within the boundary of the meeting hall and under the jurisdiction of the Senior Men. As these changes were never reported to any authority, nothing was done to right these wrongs.

We had attended one weekend for our regular meeting and saw that the family was no longer on the back row. We never saw them again. Once a family had been sent away from the Community, it was as if they had never existed. We knew better than to ask our parents what happened, but we knew it wasn't a good thing - we knew that the family would not have chosen to leave, we knew that they had been banished. This was because of a few moments of forgetfulness on the part of an elderly lady trying to do her best for her extended family. That she may have been suffering an undiagnosed illness, maybe a form of dementia, wasn't considered. It was considered by other Community members that the family should have cared for her more effectively; in reality, this meant that the children's mother would have been responsible for both grandmothers and her own children, as her husband would have been out working. Retirement was not known in the Community - people worked until they became incapacitated by illness, injury or they died. As time moved on and they were compelled to work more slowly by their failing health, the younger people gradually took over, but no leisure time was afforded by anyone. It was very apparent that an easy life was only possible by the positive behaviour of those around. It was extremely easy for people to be reported for very slight misdemeanours as a way of encouraging others to attempt perfect behaviour. Examples were made of minor transgressions, and the fear of public humiliation at a meeting was enough to ensure that most people toed the line. The most likely people to report of others, were the women. They would report of other women who went out in public carelessly dressed, or those who attracted attention. Trust was an issue, as to be known to witness poor behaviour but not report it was as bad as behaving badly oneself.

As I was now living in a school, I had to be aware of many different ways in which Outsiders lived their lives. The constant spoken interaction between everyone, not just the 'thank you' that I had first noticed in the hairdressers, but opening doors for each other, the 'excuse me' as people reached across each other at times and, of course, the constant 'sorry'. Sorry for bumping into someone, nearly bumping into someone, and for someone bumping into me! I was adjusting well, and loved the opportunities offered for learning. After I had fulfilled my cleaning duties, I could shower and change out of my overalls, and then I could read the books in the library. I was getting to know some of the teachers quite well, and they would let me know if a certain subject in which I had expressed an interest was going to be covered in a particular lesson and, if the conditions were right, I was allowed to sit in the back of the classroom and listen to the lesson.

Breakfast over, I attended to my cleaning duties, this time I was scheduled to clean the changing cubicles around the swimming pool. Each one had a wooden door, with a mirror attached to the back which I had to remember to clean. Twenty cubicles meant twenty benches, forty clothes hooks, twenty bamboo duckboards and twenty mirrors - I had to remember to clean every item, before I could collect my dictionary and go to my desk in the library. Sitting down, I resumed reading the book about genetics. This was fascinating. It explained about how characteristics were passed from generation to generation. The chapter about eye colour in humans was really very interesting. I read of dominance (in an unusual way from how I had previously experienced this word) and recession. I read of how brown eyed parents could have blue eyed children, which amazed me. Blue eyed parents could have blue eyed children. But not brown eyed children. My parents had blue eyes. I had blue eyes. All my brothers and sisters had blue eyes. Except my blonde sister. She had brown eyes. I read the paragraphs repeatedly. I went to the shelves and looked for more books about genetics. Reading the chapters on eyes brought me to the same conclusion again and again. My blonde sister could not be the child of my parents. I remembered her being born. By that, I mean I remember her arriving at our house: my mother had gone away for a few days and returned with a baby. I had been five at the time, at school, and my older sister and I had stayed with one of my mother's sisters whilst she had been away. My brothers and other sister had stayed with another of my mother's sisters and my father had remained in the family home during our absence. He had eaten with one of the sisters each night until my mother returned home, he wouldn't have cooked his own food, men didn't do that. All the households were within a mile or so of each other, our Community tied itself together very strongly. I was confused. My blonde sister, the one whom I loved to comb my hair dry as she was much gentler than my other sisters, could not be my full sister. She must be my mother's daughter though, as my mother had definitely been expecting a baby. This could only mean that she could not be my father's daughter. The implications of that thought were too great to consider. I replaced the books on the shelf and, taking my dictionary, returned to my room. I had another hour or so before lunch, and after lunching my cleaning duties would resume. I changed my shoes into heavier ones and left the school buildings for a walk.

  I walked along the footpaths through the parkland of the Hall, these parks now mainly supported playing fields, although some acres were rented to local farms, so there were a few fields containing cattle, sheep and, much to my surprise when I arrived at Hornbeam Hall, llamas. I knew these animals to be non-threatening, and walked along the footpaths with my head down, checking I didn't tread in any of their squelchy mess. I had experienced the pungent squish of a cow pat once, and the laborious and unpleasant cleaning processes that had ensued, repeatedly cleaning off the mess from my shoes until the staining and smell was reduced to being almost invisible and undetectable. I took much more care on my walks now and, although the pathways were open to the public due to centuries-old covenants, other walkers were rare so I felt sure that I could think in the open air without fear of interruption. I strode through the fields, my agitation seemed to be fuelling a longer stride than my usual pace. Due to this I reached the woods much sooner than I had expected. I pushed past some of the fresh growing bramble stems to reach a fallen beech tree at the very edge of the wood. It had fallen along the boundary fence, breaking several spars as it did so and, although the fence had now been repaired, the trunk had remained. It may yet be sawn up for firewood, or it may stay to house the many beetles and bugs that seemed to thrive in decaying wood. Already there were small patches of colourful fungi growing, they almost resembled flowers from a distance, but I sat well clear of these, not wanting to earn myself another technical laundry session. The main trunk was sound, although it had started to crumble slightly at the lower end, where it had broken through the ground. It was as if the tree had tipped over, rather than snapped higher up the trunk. The lacey doily effect of the roots unnaturally exposed to the sunshine had become more noticeable as the weather washed the soil back to the ground. I felt the bark under my hands as I settled myself for a few minutes, it was smoother than the oak trees of my schoolyard, dry to touch as it had been a few days since we had had any rain. I gazed ahead at the honey-coloured cattle grazing as they stepped slowly across the fields. Every now and then they lifted their heads, flicking their ears as they tried to rid themselves of the ever-pesky flies, chewing rhythmically they surveyed their surroundings before lowering their heads to secure a further supply of grass. I sat there quietly for several minutes and thought about the knowledge I had gained that morning. Could that really have happened? Could my mother really have had a baby that had had nothing to do with my father? I slowly moved my gaze as I considered, focussing on the gateway at the other side of the field as I would soon be returning that way.

A woman was opening the gate, she waved to me 'Mary, Ma-ryyyy...' her voice rang out as I stood up and ran towards her, back down the path. It was one of my colleagues. Sally seemed to be a nice lady, but a little too inquisitive when making conversation with me. I had wondered why she would be so interested in learning where I had lived, worked and been on holiday, who my brothers and sisters were, and did I have a dog? There were so many questions to be answered and I couldn't see a reason why. So, I had been careful about what I said when I was around her. She seemed keen to seek out more details than I was comfortable to offer. So far, I had been able to maintain my cover, Libby had encouraged me to regard my own thoughts, feelings and history as personal information and, as such, no one else had any right to demand that for their interest. Sally had obviously followed me, and I realised as I approached that I would be questioned about the reasons behind my solitary departure. I decided to take control and greeted her as I got closer.

'Isn't it a glorious day? The trees look amazing, don't they?' Thus wrong-footed, Sally could only agree with me, and we walked back to school together chatting about the beauties of Nature. Upon my return I ran up to my room to change for my next cleaning shift; I had to eat lunch first, then I was rostered to clean all the gymnasium changing cubicles ahead of the inter-school sports competition which would take place over the weekend. As today was Friday, I would be able to take the next day off, so long as I was back at school for Sunday evening. I had arranged to go to Libby's for the weekend, and I was going on my first ever train ride! Libby had bought my ticket and sent it to my phone, it all seemed quite confusing, but we had spoken at length, and I had the relevant screenshot saved to the correct part of my phone. I would pay Libby for the ticket, using my banking app! This was a process I would do under her supervision, as there were limits to her patience and ability to instruct me in technological processes by telephone!

Preparing my shoulder bag to accompany me on another trip brought back a few memories, but I blotted them out as I chose underwear, a t-shirt and my washing things, I used the orange and red bag from Libby on that first day to hold my hairbrush, toothbrush and the like, it had been the first thing I had been given outside the Community and I loved it for its symbolism. This time I knew I would be returning, unlike the last time when I knew nothing except that I was leaving for a future. Such a lot had happened in those few weeks, my previous life in the quiet, dark house seemed to have happened to a different person. As I had prepared last time, I had only been able to take the absolute minimum - I had had to be sure that no one could see what I had put in there. No one from the Community ever questioned a girl carrying a bag, as it was possible she was carrying sanitary pads, which were never referred to by anyone, and certainly should never be seen by men. It was fair to say that the girls didn't really understand the meaning of a period, and boys would certainly not be encouraged to enquire or speak of the process. I had therefore been able to carry my bag to that final church meeting without suspicion. This time there was a much lighter feeling, I had no need to hide anything, I could include what I needed for an overnight trip and set off openly. I would catch the bus to the nearest station and take two trains to Market Wenton, the town where I had created my own look those few weeks ago with Libby. She would collect me from the station and drive me back to her house. I was looking forward to seeing her, I could perhaps ask her about the knowledge I had gained about my blonde sister.

Freedom

Stepping onto the train late that afternoon, I found a seat and sat down. My heart was hammering in my chest, and I was fighting to control my breath. I had done so many things for the first time. Got on a bus, bought a bus ticket, spoken to people I had never met, walked to a place I had never been to before, navigated my way around a railway station, found the right platform and spoken to the people on the ticket desk. They had told me to scan the ticket on the gate and it would let me through. I had tried and tried, and it hadn't worked. Eventually someone in a glowing yellow jacket had appeared from an office and had come to my assistance as a queue was building up behind me and for a moment, I thought I had recognised PC Singh. As soon as the man had spoken, I realised that it wasn't PC Singh, that it couldn't possibly be him, as he was a policeman at work in a different county, and this man was a railways' employee merely wearing a similar high visibility jacket for his own security and safety. He was very helpful and explained that it seemed that I hadn't moved the phone quickly enough and the screen had gone blank in between me finding the ticket and moving the phone to the scanner. I would have to change the settings, apparently. Another thing to ask Libby.

The people who had been delayed by my confusion had rapidly overtaken me, and I felt their irritation at being delayed. Particularly from the young man who had spoken as he passed by, I hadn't understood the words he had said, but his venom was unmistakable. Sitting on the train I took a few deep breaths and felt my heartbeat slow down. The people around me glanced up but soon returned to their phones. I was relieved, as I didn't feel up to a chat with anyone, far less a stranger wanting to know where I was going or any other information. I watched the world chug past as we set off, then the embankments, buildings and fields started to slide past more quickly until they were flashing by. I wondered how the other passengers weren't fascinated by this, the variety in our surroundings was something I couldn't take for granted. After seeing the same things day after day, and the same people too, anything new was a distraction to me. I watched and listened as we flew along the tracks, the rhythmic ker-chunk, clickerty, clickerty, clickerty, ker-chunk of the train wheels was helping me to relax, and I could hear people further along the carriage having conversations with invisible contacts.

'I'm on the train! We're going to be a couple of minutes late, but I'll see you there. No, I haven't brought the sprockets, I'll need to have them biked up.' I pondered on what sprockets were, and what biked up might mean, then my attention as caught again, by a deeper voice this time.

'No, shush, I've told you. I can't get that sorted.... Well, that's not my fault, I've tried to get tickets.... Well, I can't help that. We can go another time. I'm not telling you what to do, ohhhh. Look, we'll talk later. Yup. Me too...'

I felt that some people weren't living the shiny lives that their smart clothes and possessions were suggesting. At least my own unnoticeable appearance and quieter behaviour would not be drawing attention. It was funny how the lessons from early childhood stayed with us - although I could now wear what I liked; I was still unlikely to deliberately attract attention! The rest of the journey passed with me watching out of the window and listening to the lives of others carrying on in their own worlds which, for a short while anyway, overlapped with my own. I managed to change trains without too much confusion, no angry young men vented their irritation to me at any rate! Soon, I was walking out of the station, searching the car park for Libby's car. A car hooted its horn, and I looked round,

Libby was standing with one foot still in a car, leaning on the top of the driver's door and waving. It was a different car from before, a green one. I went over to her, and she stepped right out of the car and hugged me.

'Hi Mary, how are you doing? You look fantastic! Do you like the car? It's Brian's, he's home now.'

We drove back to their cosy little house, and she told me that Brian had returned from his secondment in the north and was back at his usual workplace. They now had two cars on the driveway, so it was a bit crowded... She rattled on with a couple more pieces of incidental gossip, then my attention was fully caught as she said that the police would be calling in during my visit.

'Why? What's happened?'

'I'm not sure, I think it's a follow up from their last visit, you know, the kidnapping thing...'

I wondered what would need to be followed up, and by the time I had dismissed the point, we were back at the house. Libby drew the green car right up to the back of her own blue car on the driveway and we got out. The front door opened, and a dark-haired man stepped into the doorway.

'Hi there, you must be Mary. Hi darling...' This was an aside as Libby kissed his cheek as she walked past him into the house.

I dangled my shoulder bag by its strap as I walked in behind Libby. 'Hi, yes, I'm Mary. You're Brian?' A few more sentences exchanged as we went through the ritual of journey details, timings etcetera as the kettle boiled and the tea tray accepted its load of mugs and cake. Libby was just carrying this into the front room when there was a knock at the door, I looked towards the door and could see fuzzy black and yellow shapes through the patterned glass. I opened it and saw two policemen standing on the step. One was the bearded man from before, the other was slightly obscured by PC Singh's big yellow padded jacket but definitely not the man from before as he had been taller than PC Singh.

'Hello Mary, may we have a quick chat?'

I opened the door wider, and PC Singh walked in, aiming for the living room from where Libby and Brian were indicating he should join us. Brian stepped back into the kitchen, and I heard him refilling the kettle. The second man walked in behind PC Singh, and I saw that the man was, in fact, a woman. She had her hair pulled back behind her head in a very tight bun. She smiled as I closed the front door and joined the group in the now fairly full lounge. The sofa was taken up with the two police people, so I perched on a footstool beside the coffee table.

'We wanted to check in on you, Mary, this is my colleague PC Martin; how are things going for you?' PC Singh asked as the police lady sat quietly and looked at me carefully.

'I'm very well, thank you.' I smiled back at him then moved my gaze to PC Martin. She smiled back but didn't say anything.

'The thing is, Mary, we've had a report of a missing person. The description is similar to yours, and also the date of disappearance matches with information we shared with you on our previous visit. But the name doesn't match. The missing person we have had a report of is not called Mary.'

I sat in silence. Libby and Brian sat silently, looking at me. I heard the hall clock ticking its unhurried seconds, as my own heart beat a hurried tempo within my chest.

'Can you help us out Mary? Does your family know where you are?'

I sat, frozen with indecision. I remembered Libby's words from my first day with her. 'We mustn't lie, but we don't need to tell all' so I answered that no, my family didn't know where I was.

Libby spoke up then, 'Mary has chosen to come here, she is free to go wherever she chooses, and she is over 18.'

'We understand that, we just needed to check on the report that we have received. What else can you tell us, Mary? Is Mary your real name?'

I opened my mouth, catching Libby's eye as I did so. 'I don't really have anything to add, I'm quite safe here, I've done nothing wrong. I am not in touch with my family at the moment.' I saw Libby frown very slightly and realised that I should probably said no more. I smiled at both the police officers. PC Martin was still looking at me, so I broadened my smile towards her. I was hoping to reassure her of my safety and encourage them to leave us alone.

In the slightly extended silence that followed, the police officers looked at each other, then stood up.

'Well, we will leave you to your afternoon then. Thank you for your time, if you want to speak to me, this is my number.' PC Martin's voice sounded familiar. I looked at her sharply. Her voice was the voice that I had heard at the traffic lights on the day I ran away. She had been the lady in trousers who had snapped at me but held onto the man running after me. I owed my freedom to her as much as I owed it to Libby. She handed me a small card printed with her name and photograph. PC Frances Martin. Her email address and telephone number were printed on there too. I held on to the card as I watched Libby close the door behind the luminous yellow jackets. Libby walked back to the undrunk tea, lifting her mug she commented that the visit had been weird. I looked at my tea and thought carefully, should I mention that PC Martin might recognise me? Would she recognise me? I had changed my appearance significantly since that moment of contact on the pedestrian crossing and I hadn't spoken. She may have heard me sobbing, but probably hadn't even seen my face. My all-enveloping coat and ugly dress were still in my bedroom, but otherwise there was nothing to connect me to that moment. I decided to say nothing, I had brought enough confusion to Libby's household and, if I told her of the connection, what good would it do?

As our visitors had now left, Brian had abandoned his tea-making and had started to cook lunch; I began to recount some of the tales from school - it was all so new to me that I had quite a few anecdotes of funny scenes around misunderstandings. I had not come across so much of the language used in a workplace, and this had made for a few moments of laughter during my time there. I was telling them both of an instance where I thought I was being asked to do some sewing and had emptied a cupboard in one of the science rooms looking for some reels of cotton when I should have been planting seeds in a pot of soil on top of the cupboard I had just emptied. And on another occasion, I had poured table salt into a glass container in a set of apparatus instead of moving the jars of chemical salt compounds from the secure cupboard to the experiment site. Confusions like this had arisen a few times and caused a laugh amongst the science staff. They were extra careful to explain what they meant more fully now, and I was gradually learning more and more. Thinking of the science department reminded me of the eye colour heredity issue again. I wanted to talk to Libby about that but wasn't sure how I felt about Brian joining the conversation. I decided to raise the topic but not include its possible relevance to my family, I wanted to develop a greater understanding of the subject in case I had misunderstood something. The idea that I may not be completely related to my blonde sister was difficult to accept.

Shadows

After slightly more than 24 hours of rest and chatting with Libby and Brian, I was packing my shoulder bag to return to school. I packed my spare clothes, and my lovely silk scarf that Libby had given me in my welcome pack. I had worn my teal jumper a couple of times and now I could include my scarf with it. I still wasn't too concerned about 'fashion', but I liked the way the colour of the jumper was highlighted by the scarf. I noticed that the dark green, oversized dress that had disguised me for so long had not, after all, been in my bedroom - I had assumed it would be there when I went to bed that first night, but I noticed that it had been washed and was now folded up into one of the carrier bags that had originally contained my new clothing. It seemed fitting, somehow, that that bag would be the method of removal for the old clothing too. I had seen the bag, in Libby's tidy little hallway containing the dress and my old coat ready for removal to a charity shop. I resolved to take it away on my next visit to Libby's. I also realised that 'my' room wasn't that at all, I would be able to use it, I was sure about that, but it was part of Libby and Brian's home, I had been visiting on my way to my new life, that was all. The room would always contain my memories of that first morning of freedom. Those memories of release, safety mixed with fear and excitement of what was to come, and I knew that those clothes had had a purpose, their purpose had been to protect me from unwanted attention, we had been told that nice girls kept themselves covered up. I was still covered up whilst wearing my jeans and teal jumper although I could walk comfortably and run without yards of thick fabric collecting around my knees. I was beginning to realise that the rules regarding our clothing had been imposed on our Community for some reasons that may be quite unsettling.

I had overheard conversations whilst out in the towns, on the trains and even in the staff rooms at school where discussions about women's appearances had been taking place. Comments about women and their appearance had led me to realise that it wasn't the clothes women wore that protected them, or made them vulnerable, but the attitudes of others. Thinking back to the times I had felt uncomfortable around certain men in the Community, how they had let their hand linger a little too long on the shoulder or waist of one of the girls - now I realised that those touches were not permitted in the Outside, the evil of which we had been warned was not awaiting us, it could very well have been amongst us all the time. Those long, voluminous dresses had not protected us from attention and the constant mantra that a girl should be nice had crushed the instinct to repulse an unwanted touch. I had seen quite young girls at my current school assert themselves in a public place and the once or twice I had been on a train I had seen girls move away from men who stood closely to them. It seemed that nice girls were very happy to say, 'Excuse Me!' in a loud, clear voice. In the Community a woman would never speak until addressed by a man, there was a hierarchy within the women too, whereby the wife of a Senior Man could address others, but the wives of less Senior Men could not. Children could address each other until they went to the Community school, whereupon the hierarchy began. I had seen sons of Senior Men addressing Classroom Mothers, but never the other way around. In Hornbeam Hall everyone spoke to everyone else.

The value of each person seemed to be recognised and the same respect was offered to and by me as to and by Mrs Higgins. The school pupils addressed all staff members as Mr, Miss or Mrs and their surname. The staff addressed Mrs Higgins as such, but other members of staff by their first names. Staff referred to others by their formal names when in the presence of the pupils. For the sake of form, I had decided to use the surname Miller. Mrs Higgins was aware of my real situation and had agreed to provide this smokescreen for me, during this term of employment within the school. Thus, the respect was maintained and my instinct to look at the floor, and to stay silent was beginning to leave me. To look at a man's face and ask him a question for the first time had taken a huge amount of strength. I had only asked him to tell me the way to the science rooms, and he had only replied 'to the end of the corridor and turn right' but it had felt as if I was screaming at the top of my voice. Attracting attention had been so very wrong for eighteen years, and here I was. Speaking. To A Man. Of course, the man in question must have wondered what on earth was wrong with me, as I had felt my face go so very red. I had spoken to him several times since, and to others too and it was no longer such an ordeal. It was surprising how quickly I had adapted to the school community and its ways. I now had confidence that I could adapt to many other ways. I knew that my time at the school wouldn't be for very long, but I was increasingly certain that I would be able to survive well at a college, or university. My education was becoming more important than ever.

  I stripped the bed in which I had lain so comfortably since I had left home - the bed at the school was comfortable too, but this room was a particular sanctuary. I folded the sheets and pillowcases which I had used, stacked them on the foot of the bed, then I carried my shoulder bag back down the stairs. Libby was going to drive me to the station; my train left at 2pm and I would need to change trains again, then find the bus that would drop me near to the school. The final part of my journey would be a very short walk to the school gates, then a long walk up the tree-lined drive. I loved that walk; I loved being part of the trees' world.

Their spreading branches, their leaves that swished so gently until the wind grew strong enough to make them scream their protests during a gale; the trunks which stood as strong as any wall until the smallest of creatures, a fungal spore, crept in and gradually reduced the huge, majestic giant to a crumbling, squishy mess. Luckily this fate had not befallen the Hornbeams, but in the woodland where I loved to walk, there were a few ash trees that had suffered this fate. They were in a progressive state of decay and had been left for nature to process as best it could. In other parts of the country, I understood that some of these trees had been burned to try to eradicate the fungus but, understandably, by the time we humans had noticed the effects, the fungus had already moved on to other trees. The only way to eradicate it was to eliminate all ash trees. Which was impossible.

Libby drove me to the station - as we approached the town, she mentioned that there may be others that could follow the same escape as I had done. The telephone number was still in the second-hand clothes shop, a favourite of the Community women, and this time it had also been left on peel-off notes, so a person could take the top one and not look around for a pen. I thought that was a brilliant idea! I asked how the shop had come into the process, and she said that the Network had various points of contact for people. The clothes shop was ideal as it was run by a charity unconnected to the Community, but so many Community women bought their clothes there, and the men rarely visited it. The volunteers who ran the shop included a sympathetic lady who had been witness to some unguarded and emotional behaviour by one of the younger women several months earlier and she had traced the Network through the neighbourhood in an attempt to find help for the desperate young woman. I wondered if the lady who had served me in the shop that time has been the sympathetic lady that Libby mentioned. She had certainly suggested she could have been - 'we're here for you' had been her words to me as she handed me the pencil and paper. The men bought new clothes for themselves, they were in businesses and needed to maintain a professional image. It didn't matter that the women were in shabby clothes, they were forever in the background. If a man needed new clothes, he would use a shop in the main shopping street, which was run by the Community, and the women would not be going there, unless to collect an item at their husband or father's direction. I was glad she still felt able to help others in the way she had helped me, and I wondered if I could help too. I said as much and Libby answered that she was glad to help and would also be glad of my help in the future but that I needed to focus on myself for a while, there were still some big steps to take.

Sitting on the train a while later, I watched the flickering countryside through the windows. Trees grew close to the track giving train passengers a fractured view of the fields beyond. Every now and then there was a gap in the trees, and this allowed a sudden vista of distant hills, fields and sometimes livestock to gaze upon before the trees reappeared and the flickering began again. My mind went back to the minute before I had boarded the train. I had been hurrying across the main road at a pedestrian crossing and glanced at the cars stopped at the lights. There had been a few cars, and the one behind the front one was a smart, black one and there were two people sitting in the front. The driver had been out of my line of vision, but the lady passenger had been clearly visible to me, and I had been to her. Our eyes had met, and she had looked at me as I crossed the road. I had glanced around as I hurried into the station foyer, and she was still watching me. Her headscarf and simple clothing suggested that she was a member of the Community. She was sitting in a typical Community car, expensive, new and dark in colour. The timing was exactly right to suggest that she was being driven from the Sunday church meeting to a family home for lunch. I hadn't realised that there were Community members in this town, but the reality was that there could be. I did know that there wasn't a meeting room for a church service, the closest one would be in my hometown.

I hurried in to catch my train and reflected on that moment of possible recognition. I knew that I was safe on my way to school, but the idea that I may have been recognised troubled me. The car was so like the one that had been at the traffic lights as I ran across the road those few short weeks ago. Was it the same one? What, if anything, had been said about my disappearance? I didn't know what happened when just one person disappeared, and I began to think of the effect that my actions may have had on my family. I had been so concerned until now of how I could look after myself, that I hadn't considered my parents or siblings. Running away could have brought disgrace, humiliation or shame on those left behind. Might they be isolated from the Community? Would there be any support for them? I wondered what I should do. I resolved to telephone them. I had my mobile phone and could remember the number printed on the centre of the circular silver disc of the telephone in the hall. Being a Sunday afternoon, it was likely that they would be at home, their position within the community meant that they would be unlikely to be at a family lunch somewhere. Standing up, I walked down to the end of the carriage. I took my shoulder bag as it wasn't long until I would need to change trains. I leaned against the rocking wall of the end of the carriage and tapped the number into my phone. I waited, eventually the telephone rang.

Contact

'Good afternoon...' My father's voice sounded familiar as I listened. My throat closed slightly, and I gasped.

'Good afternoon!' He spoke again, a little louder.

'Hello, Father. It's me.' There was silence. Then his voice came again, harsher in tone now. 'How dare you. How DARE you! Your actions have ruined us. Don't call again.'

There was a click, and the line was dead. I redialled; the engaged signal sounded. The train slowed and the announcer spoke in peculiarly clear tones of the station approaching and I prepared to leave the train. My whirling thoughts confused me slightly as I stepped off the train and turned to make my connection. Walking along the side of the train I thought over his words. I had ruined them. This must mean that people knew I had gone. Those men who had followed me had obviously connected me to my family. They must have followed me from the meeting room. I went over and over in my mind how they may have seen me leave, who may have seen me at what time and who may have spoken to whom about me. This was the level of fear that had ruled me and others in the Community.

'Hey, Miss...' I looked up and realised I was at the end of the platform. The train was moving beside me and instead of the stairs over the track to the next platform, I could see the tracks disappearing into the distance. I turned to see a man in a bright yellow vest waving to me, I acknowledged his shout with a wave and retraced my steps, this time towards the stairs that would take me to the appropriate platform for my connecting train. I walked past the man, saying to him that I was miles away.

'Too right, you nearly were!' he said.

I pulled my attention back to my journey and ran up the steps. Focussing on the moment rather than my thoughts, I made the second part of the journey safely and was soon walking to the bus stop from where I would get the bus back to the school. I walked along the high street, past some shops and stepped aside to allow a young woman to pass beside me. As I did so, I glanced at her and recognised the tired face of my sister. My older sister, who had been set to marry. What was she doing here? I spoke her name and she jerked her head round to see me looking at her. We froze, looking at each other.

'What are you doing here' I asked, 'what has happened?'

'I got married', she said. She looked at my clothes, then back at my face, noticing my lipstick, noticing my shorter hair, held with a scrunchie. 'Why did you go? What have you done?'

At that moment a tall, smartly dressed man approached and took her arm.

'We must go. Dear. Excuse us please.'

They walked away, she glanced once over her shoulder at me, then resumed the pose I knew so well, downcast eyes and silence as she walked meekly beside the man who still had hold of her arm. He must be her husband. She hadn't looked pleased to see him, but that was the reality of Community life. She accepted him, as all women were expected to do. She would look after his house, bear and nurture his children, accompany him to church meetings and attend to his wants and needs. I didn't know if he had a business, I expected that he did, so she would maybe work there too. I knew that she would be quizzed on why she had spoken to me. To speak to a stranger was not allowed, especially in a street. He wouldn't have recognised me and may not even know of my existence. Were she to explain about me she may well be at risk of punishment. Would she risk lying to him? He must know about me; my father had just told me of the ruination I had caused. That must mean that my departure was public knowledge. At least it hadn't prevented her marriage. Marrying into a disgraced family wasn't an ideal situation and I wondered about the husband's background, he was not likely to be from a high-ranking family and may even have his own challenges to overcome. I hoped my sister had the strength to say that she hadn't known me. I got onto the bus feeling frustrated with the whole situation. How was it right that people could have such a harmful effect on so many others? The Outsiders were so much happier than the Community, from what I had seen in the school anyway. I wondered what I should do. Walking up the hornbeam avenue a little later, I decided that I needed to continue with my job and work out my plans for university.

  I got back to school in time for the staff supper. Shepherds' pie and vegetables. Followed by apple sponge and custard. I ate heartily and then went for a stroll around the fields before the sun sank and the evening chill drove me inside. Scrubbing the changing cubicles in the swimming pool building later, I remembered the look in my sister's eyes. Her wedding would not have been the lavish affair that I had heard some of my new colleagues describe, I heard of elaborately decorated tables, cakes and dresses; I saw dozens and dozens of photographs of huge numbers of people all eating together, and dancing. It all looked amazing, and I wondered how it felt to dance, to wear such elaborate clothing, and to wear such beautiful hats! The couples I had seen in the photographs shown to me on mobile phones were smiling, kissing, holding each other. I had heard stories of how the participants had met, how they had dated, fallen in love, lived together and then chosen to marry each other. My sister would have had a short ceremony, repeating the official wording from the Outsider official, and this would take place in the usual meeting room in the town where her husband lived. My parents may have been present, as they would have driven her, with her luggage, such as it would have been, down to her new home that day. His parents would probably have been present, but there would have been no need for my parents to establish a relationship with them. As a bride, she had left the family to live elsewhere. Maybe there would still be contact with her birth family, should a child be born to the couple, the mother's family would visit, maybe stay for a few days in their home.

Community members were not allowed to use hotels. Never should we sleep or eat under the same roof as Outsiders. Coffee shops, restaurants, cafés were all forbidden to us. We could buy ice creams from a van and eat them away from others, we could prepare picnics and distance ourselves from the other families enjoying a beach or the countryside. Running in and out of the sea like so many other shrieking children was forbidden, usually we hadn't learned to swim, as this wasn't seen as seemly. Wearing the necessary clothing in public would be wrong, close contact with Outsiders would be uncomfortable at least and improper at best. Community children would be allowed to run barefoot on the beach, but not to wear shorts, or swimwear. Toy spades and the like wouldn't be included in such a day trip, maybe a kite would be packed, but usually merely a sandwich picnic and drinks. The freedom of the beach would be the delight of the children, and likely to be on a weekday as weekends were so taken up with church meetings. I had faint memories of a day by the sea, we had been to a beach and had a picnic once when I was very young, before I had started school.

I could remember the sound of the waves and the feel of the frothy seawater around my bare toes as I had walked along the water's edge, holding my father's hand. I had no memories of where we had gone, or why, or how we had got there, but we had never been back. I had heard the children of the Senior Men talking of family trips they had taken, school play times were the only time such conversations had taken place, and the photographs that I had seen in those geography lessons had included coastal scenes.

In fact, I had recently seen photographs of a colleague's family friend who had got married on a Mediterranean beach a few months earlier. So very different from what my sister would have experienced. No friends, no speeches, no colour, neither flowers nor champagne! Her usual clothes and, instead of an elaborate hairstyle, her usual hairband or headscarf. We were encouraged to leave our hair uncut, but were allowed to wash it weekly, and brush it daily. Anything more was considered vanity, which was seen to be sinful. My hairband had been a compulsory part of my dress for my whole life, from babyhood. Previous generations of the Community women had had to wear a neutral-coloured headscarf, to cover their hair. That I and my sisters had always worn these wide, elasticated hairbands as a hair covering was regarded by some of the older women as scandalous, as our ears and necks could be seen. Their disapproval was definitely felt by us, but as the rest of the girls our age in the Community all wore hairbands, we endured the glares with the patience we had had so many hours of church meetings to practice.

I wondered about my geography teacher, who had left the school so suddenly all those years ago - had she married her fiancé? I hoped so, and that she was now teaching other children in a school which recognised her talents and appreciated her kindness. Switching out the light I lay, sleepless, as I remembered the resigned, defeated look on my sister's face. Where was she living? Could I contact her again? The night birds called as the darkness deepened. My open window allowed the cool air to refresh the room, and the calls of the owls drifted across from the woodland. Apparently, a nightingale sometimes sang, and once a nightjar had been recorded. I left the window open every night once I had heard of that, I would love to hear either of those birds. I resolved to ask the English teacher who had mentioned them, to find out more about the sound of the songs, I needed to know what to listen for. Eventually I must have slept, as suddenly the sun was streaming in, and my phone alarm sounded a command to start the early cleaning. Science laboratories again today - always a source of interest!

Secrets

As half term approached, I realised that I was quite enjoying the routine and structure of the school timetable. I worked hard during my shifts, cleaning and returning the scattered equipment to their rightful places. I had affixed lists to the inside of the cupboard doors, detailing the required contents, which helped me remember what had to go where. Apparently, some of the more scatter-brained teachers were glad of these lists too! Their focus on the subject rather than the preparation and housekeeping issues of the room meant that equipment was abandoned or shoved into a nearby cupboard. With my lists, it made the search for fresh equipment easier. I didn't mind, the science staff had been so friendly and eager to share their passion of the experiments, the observations and theories, that I was just glad to be in such a positive environment.

The eye colour situation was still in my mind though. I resolved to ask one of the teachers. I had managed to discuss it slightly with Brian and Libby, but I hadn't really learned any more than what I had already discovered. It seemed likely that my blonde sister was not from my father. I couldn't imagine what could have happened. I managed to raise the point one morning, as I washed and dried dozens of test tubes. Usually these would have gone into the dishwasher, but it had seized up following a particularly messy experiment involving some sort of gel. It was assumed that the gel had blocked the drainage pipe and we awaited the attention of the janitor team. One of them would come along to attempt a flushing out procedure. Until then, I was washing the racks of tubes by hand. There was a member of staff from the biology department standing further down the workbench from my sink, she was attempting to catch locusts out of the main enclosure tank and encase each one in a smaller box. These would then be euthanised in a gas chamber and subsequently distributed to a class of biologists for dissection purposes. I didn't like the idea of that but understood that the learning had to take place. At least the creatures were well looked after during their short lives, and the gas which ended their brief existences was effective and swift acting. The grasshopper-like insects succumbed to the substance without movement, they appeared not to suffer, but I didn't like the process. I focussed on my washing task as I started to chat about the books I had been reading. The conversation developed and I was able to focus on the eye colour genetics after a while.

'Oh, yes, that's quite an interesting subject. We have to be careful covering it in school as some pupils have complex family situations. We write to the parents with regular newsletters anyway, but we make a point of writing specific correspondence about how we will be covering this topic. Imagine if a brown-eyed pupil discovered a flaw in their blue-eyed parentage in this way!'

'What do you mean?' I couldn't believe my luck; this was the exact question I had wanted to ask!

'Well, two blue-eyed parents cannot produce a brown-eyed child. Ever. It has been used in a court case to determine an inheritance issue - before DNA fingerprinting was possible, obviously. A school biology lesson is NOT the way to discover you're adopted, or that your mother had an affair!'

'Never? Are there no cases of exception? It would be a difficult message to take in as a child or teenager, wouldn't it?' I was trying to keep my voice steady.

'No, there are no exceptions.'

I could feel my heart beating faster. I began to feel hot, so I dried my hands and moved away to get another drying rack for the test tubes. They looked like enormous, sparsely bristled hairbrushes, and the tubes were put upside down onto the 'bristles' to drain. I could then put the whole rack back into the cupboard, they could drain fully, and this way avoided breakages too. I slotted the dripping tubes onto the rack, feeling myself calm down a bit as the locust-catcher had resumed her commentary on the task in hand rather continuing her focus on eye colour! I listened with half an ear to the chat about locusts. How could my blonde sister not be my father's daughter? Did he know? What had happened? My mind raced as I pushed the spiky bottle brush into the tubes, twisting it briskly to force out all the sediment from the last experiment. Anything remaining could affect the outcome of a future experiment, so I had to be sure they were clean. The repetitive task allowed my thoughts to drift off into who else may have been involved in my sister's beginning. I tried to think of men I knew who had brown eyes, further conversations had taken me away from hair colour as I understood that sometimes blonde children became dark haired adults regardless of eye colour, so I decided that I needed to narrow down the field of eye colour. It was difficult to think of brown-eyed men, as 'good' girls we didn't look men in the eye, so I tried to think of other brown-eyed children instead. I had noticed a few, one of my mother's older sister's children, and two of her younger sister's children. I could remember some of the children at school had had brown eyes, one had been the son of a Senior Man, and two more girls I could remember had brown eyes too. Of course, there were likely to be more, but I couldn't think of them instantly. I racked my brains to try to remember the colour of my uncles' eyes. I couldn't remember, as such routine segregation meant that picturing such a detail was impossible.

Returning all the racks to the cupboard, I continued with cleaning the floor and considered the other bit of news - my older sister's marriage. Even though I had only lived away from my family for a few weeks, I knew that I would be making a successful life for myself away from them. Whether I got married or not, to whom and when, would be up to me. I thought of my sister. She had a life of dependence and servitude ahead of her. I wondered how I could get in touch, who her husband was, where they were living... I decided to ask the study support team to let me use a computer, and I would search the Internet for information. Surely records were kept of marriages. I knew that although our Community marriages were so low-key, they were legal, and that the registrar would be obliged to keep proper records. I made mental notes, as I mopped, of what to search for; marriage records; Community meeting houses in the local town; future employment. I knew that this job was only for a term, and that I would need to find another paid role within a couple of months. I wanted to develop my learning, I wasn't sure I would get to university, but I would strain every sinew to make the best (albeit rather belated) start for myself. I was determined to make up for lost time and if I could bring knowledge to my sisters, then that would be even better.

Knowledge

I flicked through the notebook with all the information I had gleaned. Page headings caught my eye; Eyes; Meetings; Certificates. I had begun my notebook when I was reading in the library about eye colour. I was now certain that there would be a different father for my blonde sister; I would only be able to be certain by asking my mother, unless I could arrange for a DNA analysis to be done on my sister and any probable father. The likelihood of an answer from either of these solutions was so remote as to be impossible. The meetings pages included the addresses of all the local meeting houses. There was one in the nearby town, where I had bumped into my older sister as I had returned from Libby's house one weekend, and three more in nearby towns. I would have to investigate. The certificates page was more of a challenge. I needed to investigate further how I could see a copy of a marriage certificate, my sister would have taken her husband's surname on marriage - another thing I thought was a legal obligation on women, but it seemed that this was merely a tradition and definitely no longer a law. Several members of staff who were married had different names from their spouses. One had even made up a new surname for herself on her marriage. Not her maiden name - that very description harked back to medieval times, in my opinion anyway. I had also watched a film about suffragettes, my first day in Libby's house had brought that word to me for the first time, and I had investigated. A DVD copy of the film had been in the school library, and I had watched it on a computer one evening. That children had not legally belonged to their mothers until a few decades prior, and that women had been actual property of their husbands until a few centuries beforehand was a huge challenge to my increasing sense of what was right. And now I knew where the 'rule of thumb' originated I knew that I would never, ever use that phrase again.

I was beginning to feel so very strongly about how these archaic practices were still being carried out in an otherwise liberal, modern world. That I, my sisters and cousins had lived under such repression was a source of building fury. That we had been lied to by those we had respected was unthinkable. But it had happened. I realised that some of the lies we had been told had not been understood to be lies. My parents, I could now see, were puppets of the Senior Men, and they in turn of the Main Authority. How the Main Authority had got away with all of this for so very long was a complete mystery to me. How had those Senior Men colluded with all of this? How had they justified to themselves that this oppression of so many was in any way acceptable? As I thought about this, I began to realise that many of the Community families were linked to other families and in some cases this dependency was mutual, far reaching and, I began to see, impossible to change.

I remembered Libby's story of how her family had just packed their essential clothing and left. Their house, furniture, even her father's mobile phone which he had drowned in the lavatory pan, had probably all been lent, gifted or bought due to Community finances. To unpick property ownership and secure deeds, to establish actual contracts for borrowing, these would be challenging processes to carry out, as to question those facilitating a house of significant size to a newly married couple was not acceptable. That Libby's father had been able to retain his car ownership document demonstrated an oversight on the part of the Senior Men in his Community. Realising that my father was indebted to his Community for his house, his job and, therefore, his family's very survival, I understood that his daily routine was one of indebtedness, appeasement, obedience and non-autonomy. I had quickly accustomed myself to autonomy. Choosing my clothes and activities had become as automatic and natural as breathing, the realisation that the people I had left behind were still so restricted was a sad one. But only sad because I knew differently now. That education could cause this sadness was a source of conflict to me. I realised that as I found out more about the Outside world and its inhabitants, I would encounter more difficult situations where I would feel more sadness about how I had been lied to for so long. In a way, my mother had been right – mixing with Outsiders **was** causing me pain. But only because I had been deceived for so long.

I continued my search for jobs. I realised that I could work quite effectively as a housekeeper and was enjoying my education which ran parallel to my tasks and duties. I had decided to see if I could do a similar role in a university, living on the premises and learning in my spare time. I had looked on university websites, on employment agency websites and eventually I had even approached an employment agency. I had discussed my situation with Libby, she had warned me of signing up with an agency as I may have to pay a registration fee, and that some agencies simply promised success and couldn't deliver on this promise. I didn't want to find that I had contracted myself to obligations that I didn't want to complete, so the best thing was for me to search for a role myself. It became apparent that the universities were not looking for individuals to be housekeepers, I would have to work for a third-party company which would carry out the cleaning, but also for other companies too. It may be that I would be cleaning at a university on one day, and in a distribution warehouse the next. I resolved to find another way. Elizabeth had noticed my preoccupation and asked if I was all right one day. I mentioned that I was trying to find a housekeeping job in a university, and it was proving to be a bit of a struggle. She had sympathised, and we had gone about our respective duties.

Half term came and I was asked if I would like to accompany some of the resident staff on a seaside bed and breakfast holiday. This was my first time away on holiday, my first time in any sort of hotel and my first time sharing a bedroom with another person who was not a sister! We had a lovely room with two single beds in it, and a bathroom attached which was really convenient. I shared my room with one of the science ladies, she was a newly qualified teacher, and I was glad to get to know her and the other staff members present a lot better. A total of six of us had driven down to the south coast and stayed in a small hotel on what was described as the Jurassic Coast. Apparently, this meant that several fossilised dinosaurs had been discovered there and the knowledge that I absorbed from a walk on such beaches was fantastic. There seemed to be unlimited learning available to me. One of the others on this break was Elizabeth; and as we scrabbled about in the squelchy, muddy sand on the beach at the bottom of the crumbling cliffs, she asked me what my plans were for the future. I explained that I would like to have a similar role in a university where I could take advantage of learning there too. We chatted at length about this, as we walked along the squelching sand as the tide went out. Tides were new to me too, I dimly remembered something about the moon causing tides from another long-ago geography lesson but realised I would have to read every information board, and attend every museum too, to top up what knowledge I had.

Elizabeth could see my thirst for knowledge was increasing by the day and said she would see if she could find anyone in her network who could help with my job search. The few days I spent with these other people were wonderful, I was really beginning to feel that I was catching up with the world. The actual subject of dinosaurs was so huge, it contradicted all the teachings that I had received from within the Community, and I realised that there was so much more to the world. I had been taught that the world had been made by God and that he had then made a man and a woman who had then populated the planet. As I found out more about the world I was living on, I realised that that just couldn't be true. There couldn't possibly be two sole ancestors for the current global population of seven billion people, and I began to realise that the book that the Community had followed was more of a collection of spiritual suggestions and guidance than a journal of fact. So much of science was indisputable, and the study of so many different areas of it was what was drawing me to a university. These few days of looking at fossils on a beach, of looking at other discoveries, preserved in museums, and set into walls and photographed onto mats, t-shirts and calendars - seeing what amazing creatures they must have been, their magnitude and the scale of them made me wonder about the world has it could have been before the time of humans. I realised that the creation of the planet was not down to a pair of hands, but due to complex combinations of elements and processes. I knew that there would be no answers to some questions, and the likelihood of more questions was huge. That I could ask questions was so liberating, and I felt the restraints of my previous life fall away.

As I sat with my companions in a cosy bistro restaurant later that evening, listening to the discussions between them, as we sipped our wine and ate tasty food, I could feel the atmosphere around me. It felt as if I was wrapped in a warm blanket, without any cold anywhere around. The sound of the music being played in the background, it seemed to be a classical piece, of strings and occasionally a drumroll, cushioned my ears from the harsher laughter from another table of young men, and I could hear Elizabeth discussing the difference between horse racing as a sport and keeping a pony as a child's pet with one of the men who had accompanied us. The other man was talking to my roommate, I could hear their conversation about the challenges of maintaining a greenhouse throughout the year. Summer seemed to be just as challenging as winter although its orientation was a significant factor. He seemed to be suggesting the manufacture of a greenhouse with rotational function and the discussion of xylem growth seemed to be a vital constituent. I remembered the mealtimes from my previous life. Sitting quietly around the table, in our dark dining room, the only conversation would be about how my father and brother were getting on at work, and the occasional direction to one of us girls to fetch more from the kitchen, or to pass something to someone. That life, still only a very few months ago, felt like one that had belonged to a different person. But that was the point, I WAS a different person now. The faces of my mother and sisters drifted into focus, I remembered their expressionless faces, their meekness and their timidity. I looked around and saw Elizabeth laughing loudly, with her head thrown back; the two men were also laughing in their respective conversations, and the other lady from our group returned from outside, bringing with her the chill of the outside evening and a hint of fragranced smoke as she settled back down at the table.

'What about you, Mary? what would you like?' Suddenly I realised that five pairs of eyes were all looking at me, and the waiter was standing slightly impatiently at my shoulder as Elizabeth nudged a menu card into my hand.

'Oh, er, this please.' I pointed at the dish listed at the top of the card. I had read through the list earlier and realised that I neither knew Eton mess from tiramisu, nor sticky toffee pudding from upside down pineapple cake, so it really didn't matter what I chose. The result would add to the adventure. I agreed that I would like Chantilly cream to accompany the dish and, taking the menu cards with him, our waiter departed. He looked about the age of my younger brother. Our admittedly short conversation had reminded me of him, and I wondered, again, how they were all doing.

Some answers

Approaching the motorway services, Elizabeth slowed the car, flicking on the indicator switch. The ticking sounded loudly in the car, as the two ladies in the back of the car had nodded off, exhausted after our coastal trip. I had loved the time away, it had been full of many firsts for me, and I had soaked up the atmosphere and knowledge constantly. Even driving in the front seat of a car was new to me, as a woman, and a child, I would not have been granted Front Seat Passenger status, my mother had occasionally driven alongside my father, but only if my brothers were not with us. I watched the signs going past, watched the cars passing us, and observed Elizabeth's actions as she drove from one lane to another, approached roundabouts and drove backwards in car parks. She noticed me looking and asked if I'd ever had driving lessons. I hadn't thought that I could drive - the thought just hadn't occurred to me. As I looked around, I could see that most of the cars around us had women driving them, there were men in passenger seats too, something that wouldn't have happened in the Community. A man would never depend on a woman like that. I considered the suggestion. There were a few more weeks left at school before the summer holidays which I could possibly use to take driving lessons, I resolved to see if I could book some as soon as I got back to school. I had several hundred in my bank account now as I had managed to pay in the money that I had brought with me when I had run away, and I had been paid a couple of times since I had been at the school. I told Elizabeth that I would arrange for lessons as soon as I could, it seemed to be a life skill which I could definitely use to my advantage. I was extremely far from owning a car, but it seemed that I could learn. She smiled in agreement, as we parked in a tatty, littered far corner of the car park, the back seat passengers woke up and we joined the throng of people drifting into the shiny, noisy building where refreshment of a sort was possible.

As we sat in the cafe area, having watery yet frothy cups of warm coffee, we chatted about the half term ahead. The two men had driven home separately from us, and conversation turned to the younger one of them. My roommate apparently had hopes of something more than friendship, she had enjoyed her time away, and felt that there may be a Spark between them... The other lady, similar to her in age started asking questions, leaving Elizabeth and I to talk. Elizabeth asked if I had had any luck looking for work for after the school term. I confirmed that I was still looking, and she started to tell me of a friend of her brothers who was looking for a housekeeper to help out in his family home in a university town. He was an academic (something to look up in my dictionary, it had received a lot of consultations since I had joined the school) apparently and had a family of three children; his wife, also an academic, occasionally had to work away at short notice at a similar university, sometimes overseas. The work would be mainly cleaning, and some childcare, but the best bit was, whilst the children were at school, I would be able to have every morning to myself. So long as I got them to their school bus stops, I would not be needed again until lunchtime, when I should do any cleaning, and then be ready to prepare a family evening meal. I would live in the family home, at their expense, and be paid an additional weekly sum as wages. I liked the sound of this, and asked Elizabeth what I should do next. Her suggestion was to meet the family, and to decide from there. The other two were still discussing how romance could be sparked between two people, and we listened as they tried to think of a way of meeting. It seemed that both women would contrive to start a conversation with him, and one of them would suddenly be 'called away' to allow them to have a private chat. I was a rather uncomfortable about this suggestion, it was a little reminiscent of the manipulation used within the Community, but I could see their point of view. It was surprising how often a phone call could be used as an excuse, particularly since it was no longer necessary to have a phone actually ring! Pretending a silent call had arrived was a good excuse to get away from an unwelcome situation. I made a mental note to remember that!

As we finished our drinks and joined the mass of people leaving the building to disperse and re-join our scattered vehicles, I glanced ahead of me and saw a young woman, in a long, shapeless dress. Flat buckled shoes and a thick hairband covering the roots of her long, slightly straggly, black hair. She was ahead of me, and I quickened my pace. I could see that she was walking slightly stooped, and behind a taller man. She looked like my sister! I hastened again and caught up with her. I touched her arm, she turned and looked at me with expressionless eyes. She glanced at the tall man, still walking slightly ahead. Then she looked back at me with tears in her eyes, before turning her pale face away and she continued trudging behind her husband. He turned as they reached the crossing to the main part of the car park. Our eyes met for a second, and the disdain that drew across his face as they did so reminded me of the meetings in the hall only a few months before. Women who looked at men were considered to be harlots, no better than any other Outsider, and considerably worse than most. His disdain could also be read as contempt. Having been brought up to believe that he himself was better than any woman, in a Community that believed that their Community was considerably better than the Outside communities, he would consider himself to be in the top one percent of the human population. The arrogance this engendered would allow his self-confidence to grow to such a level that he would positively grow a new business, especially if he followed the advice 'offered' by his financial backers, successful businessmen from the Community.

My sister followed him across the car park to a dark blue car, of the luxury type favoured by Community men. I couldn't see the registration number, but saw my sister get into the back and the car slid silently forwards and away. I wondered why they had been in a motorway service station. It was possible it had been for a business reason, although I dismissed that as an option as she would not have accompanied him, I guessed it had just been for the bathroom, the cafés would not have been an attraction as eating and drinking outside the Community was not allowed. I had never visited a motorway services area whilst in the Community, and I wondered about her situation as I returned to Elizabeth's car. I sat in the passenger seat again and typed blue SUV into the notepad app in my phone, before re-joining the conversation about the half term ahead. Swimming was now the subject, another skill I needed to develop. I had splashed around in the pool, watching the others around me and trying to copy how they swung their arms and kicked their legs. I could cover some distance, probably not as elegantly as others, but enough to probably help me in a tricky situation. I decided that I'd practice as much as I could in the remains of the term. My bathing suit had been such an unfamiliar garment that I had felt almost naked when I first swam, until I realised that everyone else in the pool was similarly attired, and no one had behaved in any bad way at all. Another lie I had been forced to grow up with, that exposing a girl's skin below the neck would cause unlimited danger for her.

I wondered about the differences between me and my sister. We had had the same upbringing, but my life seemed to pivot on that long ago moment of conversation with my geography teacher. My sister may have had the same teacher but would have been in a different class and had definitely not had the same conversation. I realised that the differences between us were now very marked, were they so great that we wouldn't be able to reconnect? I was aware of other people having very close family relationships, mainly due to shared experiences. I had, necessarily, had very specific shared experiences with my sisters, but we hadn't the emotional awareness to see that we were in a traumatic situation. It was only since leaving that I had seen it for what it had been. Despite my recent departure, I felt that I now actually belonged to the world. My sisters may not be able to understand, but I felt that I needed to make contact to let them know how things could be. I wasn't sure how to work this out. But I felt that I should let them see the Outside world for what it was.

The following week passed quickly by; my work shifts, and swimming sessions kept me busy, and I had enrolled for driving lessons too. They would start the week after, and I had booked three sessions a week to begin with. As my work shifts allowed me to have time to myself in the middle of the day, I could book in my first few lessons at a quieter time on the roads. I would book in subsequent lessons at busier times and gain experience in that way. I knew that I would have to take a theory test too, and I was glad to keep busy as a way of displacing my worries about my sister. The driving lessons started and to begin with the driving was along quieter roads in and around the residential avenues in the nearby town. I learned about starting the car on slopes, turning corners right and left - this had always been a challenge for me, mixing right and left had been something that had happened from my very earliest days, earning criticism from other Community mothers and some teachers. The competitiveness amongst the Community women was such that any opportunity to denigrate another family's child was taken, it really was a Community that worried about what people thought of each other. Consequently, if I mixed up my right and left, I was mocked, and other women and children would laugh at me. In the car, beside my driving teacher, it was a bit better, I was able to think more quickly now, as I didn't feel as anxious as I had on previous occasions where a reaction was required to such a request. I could even write an L on the back of my left hand apparently, but I hoped very much not to need to do that.

I was enjoying the learning I was undertaking, and these little achievements meant a lot to me. I had always tried my best at everything that came my way and feeling the encouragement that was part of this positive environment had opened my brain up to so much potential success. Every time I felt the glow in my chest that followed an achievement, however small, I felt as if I grew a little more. I booked in for my theory test and the librarian at school helped me to access the relevant websites for the information I would have to learn, and the practice tests that were also available. I had a couple of weeks to get up to speed with the process, then I would have to go into the town to sit the test. It all seemed very sensible, and I learned as many of the road signs as I could, all the symbols seemed to make sense - apart from a really worrying one showing a car plunging into water. I hoped I'd never see that sign whilst driving. I was also intrigued to see that there was a sign for a minimum speed in certain circumstances. I thought I'd better develop my awareness of that possibility. It was bound to come up if I ignored it!

It had been some time since I had been in touch with Libby, and I wondered how she was getting on. As she also worked in a school, I knew that she would be busy, so I thought the best thing to do would be to send her a text message. It had been a little while since I had used my mobile phone, I had telephoned the driving teacher, but other than that I hadn't touched it at all. I could see that the screen was completely blank, indicating that battery was drained, so I plugged it in, the screen lightened immediately, and I could see the symbols showing that I had missed a call, and that I had received several text messages. I looked to see who had called me, but it was a number I didn't recognise. I had so few numbers in there anyway, just the one for Libby, and her boyfriend, and the driving teacher. I opened the text message section. I was supposed to remember to call it an app, but I was still getting used to that, and saw three messages had arrived from the same unknown number that had called. I opened the first one. 'Hi Mary, how are you doing? I've missed seeing your lovely face around here, let me know when you're around and I'll take you out for lunch. See you soon. H xxx'

I was puzzled. And a little worried. Who was H? Why were they missing me, and what a strange comment about my face...

I opened the next one. 'Hey, Mary! Are you ignoring me? That would be rude, and a pretty girl like you shouldn't be rude to people, especially those who rescued you from a fate worse than death. I need to see you, you're so pretty now, and really grown up. I know you must be ready to be a proper woman now. Call me. H xx'

I knew now that this must be Hector. I supposed that he had rescued me. I couldn't work out what he meant. He'd said something about my face again, and I was bewildered about the final comment about being a proper woman. I was a bit worried about the bit about being rude to him. I didn't think I had been rude, what had I done that could be rude? I supposed that he thought that I had ignored the first message, which had been sent the day after I had rung the driving teacher, and this one had been sent several days later. I didn't like the thought that I had been rude, and felt my throat tighten as I swallowed nervously. I wondered about looking at the next message and decided that I would go down and eat first, as it was almost dinner time, and face it afterwards. I left the phone in my room and ran down the stairs to the dining room. I still sometimes forgot to call it the refectory.

I joined the queue, and as I reached for the plates of food, lasagne and lemon mousse, I recalled the messages. Had I been rude? What had I done? Should I have been more grateful to my rescuers? That I might have been rude was a real worry for me. I was so preoccupied that I knocked my tray on a pillar as I turned to walk to the blue tables. As I did so, I saw one of the plates slide to the end of my tray and my lemon mousse crashed to the ground with an echoing clatter, splattering mousse across the floor. The chatter in the room silenced momentarily but resumed almost immediately as the members of staff caught the eyes of some of the pupils. They were encouraged to turn a blind eye to such public accidents. If something happened to someone nearby, pupils were taught that they should help with picking up spilt items, and to avoid treading in mess. So those children around me were walking in a big circle around the splattered mousse, and I stepped away and placed my tray on a nearby table as I reached for the plate, luckily still intact, but very sticky. A member of the catering team had appeared with a mop and bucket and swiftly mopped up the mess. I placed the plate back onto the counter, and the smiling face of Delma handed me a fresh plate of mousse.

'All right, Mary love?' I forced a smile and nodded.

'Yes, thank you Delma.' I picked up my replenished tray and, thanking the lady who had mopped so effectively, walked to the back of the room and sat at a spare place at the blue tables. I started to eat, then became aware of Elizabeth sitting down beside me. She ate her meal and, as we both finished our main courses, turned to me and asked if I was OK. I nodded and smiled. She looked me in the eyes, put her dinner plate back onto her tray and took up her spoon in preparation of eating her own dish of lemon mousse.

'Come on. Let's eat these, then go for a coffee in my office. How about that?' I said that would be great and relaxed a bit. 'It looks as if there's something on your mind Mary, am I right?' I looked at my plate, at the half-eaten mousse and said that yes, something was on my mind - I'd had a couple of messages that I didn't understand. 'On your phone?' I nodded. 'Bring it to coffee, we can look at them if you like. No pressure but bring it in case.' I trusted Elizabeth, so thought that this was a good idea.

Sitting in Elizabeth's office, with the green plants trailing from the windowsill, I pressed the buttons to call up the messages I had read just before dinner then put my phone on the table. Elizabeth put a frothy coffee in front of me, in a mug with Thank God I'm Fabulous printed on it, I briefly thought of the meeting room and the way that God was mentioned there - never had we ever thanked God for such a thing and sat in the opposite armchair with her own mug stating that she was The Best Teacher Ever. Elizabeth smiled.

'So? What happened?'

I took a sip of coffee and told her of the messages that had come to my phone, and the missed call from the same number. I read the actual words out loud, and Elizabeth frowned.

'Is this someone you know well, Mary? I am a bit worried about some of the language used.'

I explained that I thought the messages had been sent by someone that I had met, who had done me a big favour although I hadn't asked him directly. I had also met him on one other occasion when he had made a comment about me being pretty when I smiled. I remembered that he had tested me on whether I had learned my phone number, so had probably noted it down then. Or recorded it secretly...

I began to feel cold, that fact that someone I had trusted had behaved so deceitfully and used such strange wording made me feel rather sick.

'Sit back and relax, Mary.' Elizabeth spoke firmly. I leaned back into the armchair. The room swung around me, and I could hear Elizabeth's voice saying my name.

'Breathe in and out Mary. In. And out. In. And out.'

I began to feel warmer, and I opened my eyes. The room was now still, and Elizabeth's anxious face was leaning over me, and she visibly relaxed as I looked at her. She sat back and asked if I was all right. I said I felt a bit funny but would be all right. Fetching a small bottle of water from her desk, she broke the seal on the cap and told me to sip it slowly. This made me feel a bit better and I started to tell Elizabeth about Hector and how I thought he must have got my number. I said there was another message that I hadn't read yet and she offered to read it with me. I thought that was a good idea and reached for my phone again. My hand shook slightly as I opened the messaging app and selected the one unopened message. 'Hi Beautiful, when are we going to meet up then? I've got a great job for a pretty girl like you, no responsibility but lots of fun and great pay. You'll love it! Let me know. H xx'

I dropped the phone onto the coffee table and seized the water bottle again. Elizabeth looked serious.

'I think these messages are definitely inappropriate, and could even be an attempt to groom you, Mary.' I was confused. Wasn't grooming something to do with being brushed? I suddenly felt very tired. There were so many wonderful things about being in the Outside world, but it sometimes felt as if I was living in a world where everyone else spoke a different language. I leaned forward and rested my elbows on my knees, supporting my forehead with my hands. I felt my eyes running and I sniffed, Elizabeth spoke kindly.

'Look, don't worry about this Mary, there are things that we can do. Does this person know where you are? We can block his number on your phone, so he can't send you any more messages or ring you, but I think it would be wise if we screen-shotted them first and then we can consider letting the police have them. Once we block him, the messages will vanish.' She put a box of tissues in front of me and patted my shoulder. 'Really, you are safe here, you know that don't you?' I nodded and blew my nose.

'What's grooming? I thought it was about being brushed?'

'Well, it can mean that, but here it means that someone is trying to gain your trust by flattering you, this is actually a bit clumsy, sometimes it is more subtle, unnoticeable, even. It's used when someone, usually a man, but not always, is trying to befriend someone, usually a woman, or even a girl, but not always, and convince her that she is his girlfriend. Sometimes the girls find themselves in quite unpleasant situations, and it can be very dangerous. I'm really very glad you told me about them. Now, let's get the screenshots done.' She showed me how to make the phone photograph what was on the screen, and how it stored the pictures. 'Do you want to keep the pictures, Mary? I don't think you should keep reading them, but I do believe a record should be kept of them.' We discussed it, and decided that I should email them to myself, and send them to

Elizabeth. We would talk about them again tomorrow and decide what to do about the police. Elizabeth then showed me how to block the number that had sent me the messages and tried to ring me too. We also took and recorded a screenshot of the Missed Calls list, which showed the date and time of the call. She walked back to my room with me, I plugged in the phone to re-charge, and switched it to silent, so I wouldn't be disturbed by it. She told me not to think about H, or the messages until the next day and we would decide what to do then. I agreed to meet her at lunchtime to talk about it and went to bed a bit earlier than usual but feeling much happier.

Next steps

As I mopped and wiped the laboratory floors and benches, I hummed under my breath, there had been a lot going on over the last few weeks and I felt a bit lighter for speaking to Elizabeth. I was going to meet with her at lunchtime, I had decided to ask for her help in reporting the messages to the police and I was relieved to have made the decision. I had slept surprisingly well and woken with a feeling of lightness. The laboratory floor gleamed in the early morning sunshine, and I took my cleaning equipment through into the preparation room - this was where the equipment for classroom experiments was assembled, where the chemicals were stored and, in one corner there were some animals kept for observation. A few small frogs in one tank, and another tank contained a pair of small mice. These were welcome additions to a lesson and the pupils enjoyed observing their behaviour. I loved seeing them, they were not handled very often, so they were in as natural an environment as possible. They would build tiny nests, sometimes against the glass sides of the tank which allowed viewers to see the cosy burrow in which the two tiny mice would cuddle together to sleep. I had been told that care was taken to ensure that the two were not a breeding pair, as they were prolific breeders and apparently there could be problems if the offspring then bred with each other. It was something I had meant to research, as it sounded interesting. I made a mental note to read about inbreeding during my next library time. I had my fourth driving lesson booked for the end of my cleaning shift and was enjoying the experience of being in control of my own transportation. Freedom felt good, and I felt the responsibility of controlling a vehicle too.

Changed out of my overalls, I ran down the school driveway, underneath the hornbeams, disturbing the squirrels as they scampered around the bottom of the tree trunks, occasionally running up the trees into the branches, and sometimes running right up to the leaf canopy. Arriving at the end of the drive I stood to one side, leaning against the rough brick gatepost as I got my breath back. Cars drove along the main road, and I was dimly aware of a tractor chugging along towards me. The driver sat high up in the cab, and I could see that there was a line of cars behind him. Some of these cars overtook the slower-moving vehicle from time to time, but the line of cars was slowly getting longer. I watched as the cars indicated and pulled out, flinching as one of them caused a car driving in the opposite direction to brake sharply and a horn sounded. It was the closest thing to an accident I had ever seen, and I felt my heart beating a little faster as the cars avoided colliding and drove their separate ways. The tractor driver drove as fast as he could past the school gates, and I looked at the cars following. I noticed a large dark blue car in the line of slower moving vehicles and I was reminded of my sister, it looked like the car I had seen her getting into at the motorway service station. I looked at the back window and met the eyes of my sister, looking listlessly out of the window. She looked right at me, but I was too far away to see if she had recognised me. Her husband looked ahead as he drove and didn't appear to have noticed me. I looked after the car as it drove past and noted the letters RKC in the licence plate but couldn't remember the numbers.

My theory test was approaching, and I took care to concentrate on everything I was told and everything I could see; pedestrian behaviour was quite a challenge - anticipating their potential actions was sometimes difficult, so I took care to keep an eye out for those particularly close to the kerb. As I pulled up at a junction, I flicked on the turning signal to show that I wanted to go left, and looked carefully both ways, checking for a gap in the traffic. As I looked to my right, leaning slightly forward, I saw my sister, walking slowly along the footpath, distinctive in her long grey skirt, long black hair and thick grey hairband. Briefly I wondered why she didn't wear the black one anymore, she had always done so at home. She walked along slowly, with her head bowed, she seemed to be looking at the floor. As I looked, she turned into a driveway of a house at the junction. Was that where she lived? I could see the name of the road I was waiting in and muttered it to myself. New Brighton Avenue. A horn blasted behind me and at the same moment my teacher spoke.

'We can go, Mary, it's clear!'

'Sorry!' I muttered as she waved apologetically at the impatient driver behind us and I turned left, driving away from the thin shabby figure. I forced myself to concentrate on the road, the signs and so on. My driving test would come along all too quickly and I would be better prepared to pass if I absorbed as much knowledge as I could.

At the end of the lesson, as I drove back to the end of the school drive, my teacher said that I was doing very well, and I should book the earliest test possible once I had passed my theory test. I was making good progress, and had several lessons a week, so I should be ready to take my test in a few weeks. I agreed and said that I would look forward to the next lesson, which we fixed for the day after tomorrow. It made for a very busy time, but I wanted to make the most of all opportunities that came my way.

As I walked up the drive to the school, I remembered the sightings I had had of my sister. In the few weeks since I had left my family, I had come a long way, and it seemed that she had too. She was now a married woman, she had a husband and a new home, but she looked so unwell, thin and subdued. She had never been a very outgoing person, none of the Community girls could be described so, but she had never looked so pale and sad. I wondered how I could get in touch with her. I had no idea who she had married, all I knew was the colour of her husband's car, some of its licence plate details and possibly where she lived. I had no proof that she was living in the house I had seen her going to, but within the Community it was unusual to go to other houses. I decided to look up the house on the map app I had on my phone and slowed my pace as I searched for New Brighton Avenue. Looking at the aerial view of the property, I could see that it was a detached house, which fitted the Community protocols. It was necessary to have as few reasons as possible to engage with neighbours, so detached properties were the norm. I looked for the house number and noted it. I had arrived back at the school buildings now, so I put my phone away and went to get changed for a swim before lunch. I was enjoying the freedom of swimming, I was now used to wearing the swimsuit; it had, at first, felt very unnatural to reveal all my limbs, but I was much more comfortable now.

  Sitting at the lunch table a little later alongside other staff members I could hear all sorts of chatter around me; something caught my ear though - 'she didn't say so, it's all a bit weird, so secretive…' I recognised the voice, it was Sally, talking to one of the science teachers. I gulped. I had instinctively known that she was very interested in people, and had taken care not to disclose too much, but I wondered why she was so interested in my life. The teacher that she was talking to didn't seem as interested, as I could hear her responding.

  'Well, it really isn't anything to do with us, is it?'

  'But don't you think it's strange? Wouldn't you think she would at least mention her family? I don't get it. I think she's hiding something…'

'It really is *nothing* to do with us, is it? She can come from Mars as far as I'm concerned, she's been interviewed and the checks must have come back ok, we really don't need to worry about her. I think she is a really nice girl, and she doesn't need to share anything she doesn't want to. Let her be, Sally.'

Sally was silent and I waited a moment before turning towards her under the guise of reaching for a water jug. Her face was bright red, and she was stacking her tray ready to return it to the counter. Her lips were pressed together, and she stood and quickly walked away with her tray. Her neighbour, who had been eating her dessert as Sally packed up, rolled her eyes and started to pack up her own tray. I did the same and caught her up as we returned our trays to the counter.

'Did you hear her?'

'I did,' I replied as we walked out of the refectory.

'Don't worry about it, Sally just likes to know everything about people, it's not just you. She used to hound another girl, who wouldn't tell her all her business, she gets sort of fixated sometimes. Keep your distance, and she will soon catch on to someone else.'

I couldn't help but think that I had caused this problem though, by being reserved I had attracted attention. I wondered what I should do. Keeping away would be the best thing to do, maybe she would forget about me, but I doubted it.

As I walked along the corridor, past the staff reading room, Elizabeth opened the door and we nearly collided.

'Oops! Oh, I'm glad I've seen you Mary, can we chat?' I nodded and we walked towards her office, passing Sally as we did so. She was still red faced and she looked up as she passed us, looking at me directly.

'Hi, Sally.' She forced a smile and muttered a brief response before walking on quickly. Elizabeth glanced at me, she missed nothing, but seldom commented. I followed Elizabeth into her office, and she closed the door as I sat in one of the armchairs. She sat down too and started to tell me that my next employer had confirmed my start date. I was to begin my new job there at the beginning of September, and I should move in with them on August 31st. She handed me some photographs and a sheet of paper detailing my new employer's personal details and a list of likely tasks.

'I think it would be nice to arrange a meeting, shall we set up a video session? That way you can meet the family - what do you think?'

'I'd like that, will you be there too?'

'I can be, if you'd like me to be...' We decided that Elizabeth would contact the family and try to arrange an online meeting for a Saturday morning. There were five weeks left of the term and I had a driving test coming up around the start of the holidays. It would be good to make contact and find out a bit more about the place where I was going to live and work for the foreseeable future. I folded up the paper and put it with the photographs in the pocket of my hoodie. Thanking Elizabeth, I mentioned the messages that we had saved yesterday. We talked about how to report these, and she suggested that she drove me to the local police station and made a complaint. I mentioned that I already had a contact in the police from my time with Libby, and it might be an idea to contact them. Elizabeth looked concerned.

'Have you had trouble before, Mary?'

'Not exactly, there was a point raised by someone at the time I went to live with Libby, and I met them at a follow up meeting regarding that. They left me their contact details, so I could email them to let them know what has happened perhaps?' She agreed and reminded me that she was always here for me to talk to, regardless of school term time or even after I had left for my new job. This was a source of comfort for me, I felt reassured and knew that I could count on Elizabeth to help me if I needed it. I hoped that one day I could be able to help others. Without people like Libby and Elizabeth, people like me would be trapped in the lives in which we had been born, with very little chance of freedom. I returned to my room, ready for an early night and to look at the paper and photographs of my new employer. As I ran up the stairs, I bumped into Sally coming down.

'Oh, hello!' I said, as she blushed bright red again.

'Hi', she muttered as she ran past me, and I heard a clattering as she descended, it sounded like a bunch of keys, but I decided that it must be coins, possibly in her pocket. I pushed open the door to my corridor and walked quickly to my room. I unlocked the door and went in. Immediately I felt cold. Something had changed. I looked around the room. My desk drawer was slightly open. I went over to where it stood beneath the window. I glanced out of the window, and saw Sally speaking to the janitor, she passed him something which glinted in the evening sun. He took something from her, as he did so he dropped it on the ground, and I heard a metallic clatter. He bent to retrieve a large bunch of keys. I watched as she walked away, around the corner of the building, towards the staff garden. I looked at my desk, noticing that it seemed a bit less tidy than usual, the books I had borrowed from the library were still stacked in the corner, but slightly over the edge of the desk. I pulled the drawer open, and looked at the papers inside, they had definitely been looked through, someone had rummaged in there, the usually smooth papers, letters from the bank and from the driving school together with my notebooks were all slightly crumpled, as if someone had pushed them about rather than taken them out of the drawer. I felt rather sick. Had Sally been in here, looking for something? Why would she do this? How had she got the keys to do so?

I ran out of my room, down the stairs and across the yard towards the janitor who had finished locking up the storage units beside the swimming pool and was now returning to the main administration block. As he put his keys back in his pocket, he looked at me and blushed slightly.

'Hi,' I said. 'Did Sally ask you for the keys?'

'That's right,' he said, 'she said that it was to drop in a parcel which had been delivered for you. Is everything all right?'

I said that there was no problem at all, and I had just wondered. Thanking each other, we wished each other a good evening and we went our separate ways.

I returned to my room, took a shower, and got into bed. Tomorrow was likely to be a busy day and the peace and quiet that I could see from the stars shining through the gaps in the evening clouds would help me to relax. I knew that my sisters, and my father and my mother would all be able to see the same stars, if they were looking, and I wondered how they were getting on. It seemed such a long time since I had seen them: I knew that my father would not want to talk to me, but I wondered about my mother.

I slept but woke frequently during the night. I kept thinking about my mother. Was she thinking of me, or was she so busy with the normal way of living that she didn't have time. Had she forgotten about me? Would she want to see me again?

Quick progress

The next week passed by in a flash. I had my usual shifts to complete, additional driving lessons and the theory test for driving had been confirmed for the Friday afternoon, following a cancellation. Whilst I was sorry for the circumstances that had taken the previous booker to hospital, I was glad to be able to get that part of the process behind me. Any spare moment I spent in the library, trying to learn what I could about the city I would be working in, and Elizabeth confirmed that the video meeting would take place on Saturday morning. I was to meet her in her office after breakfast and subsequently we would all talk and establish arrangements for the summer. I was quite excited about this; it heralded the beginning of my own life. Where I could make my own future decisions. I was living in a controlled environment at the moment, with a lot of responsibility for my own actions and decisions, but the shelter and structure of the school situation encouraged a limited amount of autonomy. I was looking forward to my new life and could see that the few weeks left of term would allow me to tie up the loose ends of research, driving lessons and swimming. I was confident enough to swim several lengths now, I felt that I could stay afloat for over a hundred meters, and this gave me confidence in the water. I knew that I could go boating secure in the knowledge that I would be safe.

The usual personal housekeeping (getting my own laundry done and shopping for essentials such as shoes) I continued with and was really enjoying my time and I set off for my Driving Theory Test on Friday afternoon as planned. I had arranged to undertake my evening cleaning shift a little later than usual, as the test was to be taken in an area of town I wasn't familiar with, so travelling could take longer than first thought. I got off the bus in the town and walked along the unfamiliar paths towards the test centre. I waited in the unfamiliar rooms furnished with plastic chairs and enormous computers – much bigger and more cumbersome than the sleek laptops which furnished the offices at Hornbeam House. There were a few other people waiting, a tired-looking woman who seemed to be quite a few years older than me, and two teenage boys who stared sulkily at their phones as we waited for the door to open. Two minutes before the appointed time, the door squealed as a short man hauled it towards him, and he read a list of names from the list in his hand. As people heard their names they stood up. At two of the names, no one moved. He read them again, slightly impatiently. I looked towards the staircase we had recently ascended to access the plastic furniture, to see if Adrian Somebody was on his way... Then I realised that the other person the short man was calling for was me! It had been so long since I had heard my real name that I had almost forgotten it and, of course, my driving licence was in my real name, not Mary Miller. I leapt to my feet and apologised, meeting his exasperated gaze with a smile. He rolled his eyes, like some of the teenagers at the school, and I showed him my learner's driving licence which allowed him to tick off my name on his list before I followed the others into the room, sitting down at the desks as instructed by Short Man. It was apparent that he did not really enjoy his role, and I could see that it may not be very exciting. I could see that he could take a little more pride in what he was doing though and improve the experience for himself and the candidates. We listened to his monotonous instructions, and I took up the mouse in preparation for the test. I was aware of the others doing the same. The computers were arranged in a circle with the screens facing outwards, a little like a flower. We all sat in the positions of the petals, with the humming computers as the collected stamens. The computers were set up so that they could all be used without anyone being able to overlook any of the other screens, each desk had dividing walls to enable privacy. The screen flickered into life, and I put on the attached headset and 'commenced the exercise'. I watched video clips and clicked through a series of multiple-choice answers through several cycles and eventually came to the final question. It was a triangular road sign showing a car tipping forwards towards a set of wavy lines. I smiled, as it was exactly the sign that had caught my attention a few weeks ago. Clicking the answer Unfenced Riverbank or Quayside Ahead rather than Car Washing Facilities Nearby or River Crossing and other similar interpretations, I sighed with relief that the test was now complete. The monotonous voice in my headphones announced that the Exercise was Over, and the words appeared on my screen suggesting I remove my headphones and leave quietly. Apparently, the results would be sent to me within seven days, so I took my leave from Short Man and confirmed my name and date of birth before he offered my Confirmation Of Completion slip for the test. I left and started down the stairs, I decided that I would walk back through the town to the bus station, and that I needed to pick up a couple of things from one of the shops I would pass on my way. I was thinking about that as I approached a main crossroads close to the row of shops I needed, and I could hear someone calling behind me.

'Audrey, Audrey, wait...'

I turned to look for traffic at the pedestrian crossing and the lady from the test centre ran up to me.

'Oh, you do walk quickly, I was trying to catch you, Audrey. I was wondering if you could recommend your driving instructor. Mine is ill and I need to find a new one, so...' She rattled on, as the crossing regulator started bleeping and we joined the other people surging to cross to the other side of the road. I thought quickly as I walked, should I just give her the instructor's number and rush off?

I wasn't keen to be making friends using my real name, so I stopped near the doorway of a clothes shop. I fumbled for my phone, and scrolled through the contacts, smiling politely as the lady, called Janice (I was learning as she continued her breathless monologue), also reached for hers. I read the number to her, and the name of the instructor and she tapped away on her phone as she continued to talk.

'I don't know if you've got time for a coffee. We could talk over some of the questions… I wasn't sure about the signs one. The one with…'

I interrupted, something I would never have done before as Audrey.

'I'm so sorry, I have to rush for a bus, lovely to meet you. Bye!' I walked away briskly, leaving her still talking. I wasn't comfortable treating her like that, but my priority was to return to school as Mary. I could hear her calling after me, I glanced over my shoulder and as I did so, I walked straight into a tall man, a man I had seen before, but not so close. I apologised automatically, and he turned to look at me. Our eyes met and I felt my heart stop beating. It was one of the Senior Men from my Community.

'Well,' he said, 'here you are! What do you think you are doing, look at the state of you!' as he spoke, he switched a bag from his right hand to his left and I stepped back as he reached for my arm. I took a huge breath, turned and ran, all I could hear was his voice, raised in rage, shouting.

'Come here!'

At the same time, I could hear Janice calling me too.

'Audrey, Audrey! AUDREY!'

I ran as fast as I could, along the road towards the bus station, forgetting about my shopping, I looked over my shoulder as I reached a corner and saw the Senior Man talking to Janice. She was holding her phone and scrolling. My heart sank as I realised that he was probably getting the driving instructor's number from her and I ran faster, away from these people. Together, one deliberately and one innocently, they could take away my newly found freedom.

I reached the bus and got on. As it drove out of the bus station, I watched out of the window, hoping that no one else from the Community had seen me. The bus stopped at another bus stop, and I saw the grey-clad figure of my sister walking slowly along the footpath, past the bus stop, making for another route's stop. She still looked very pale, and her downward gaze meant that it was difficult to see her face, she looked up slightly as she sidestepped to avoid a pushchair being pushed towards her. She looked at the baby in the pushchair and her hand moved to her stomach. Maybe that was the point, maybe she was pregnant! That could explain her pale appearance and her tired look. Just then the bus revved its engine, and she looked up as the doors closed with a squeaky sigh. She looked right at me. I smiled. She stared and her mouth moved very slightly. I turned to continue to look at her as the bus drove off, she gazed after the bus, still with her hand on her stomach. The bus turned a corner, taking me back to school and she was lost to my sight. I thought hard as I sat on the bus, lurching round corners, I grabbed onto the handrail in front of me. It was slightly sticky, as if a small child had been clenching their jam-laden hands around it, and I resolved to wash my hands as soon as I got back to school. My shift would be starting immediately on my return, the gym changing rooms, and then the pool changing rooms all awaited my mop and disinfectant bucket. I would be missing my chance to swim today, but I'd get more chances in the final few weeks of term. Tomorrow was my online meeting with my new employers. Things were certainly moving on for me!

Waking early the next morning, I lay and listened to the early morning sounds from the birds in the trees around the school buildings. The hornbeams made up the avenue approaching the main buildings, and then there were several mature trees surrounding the cluster of buildings. None were close to the walls, but the outlook from most of the windows included at least one large tree, I guessed that the colours in the late summer would be beautiful, as the trees began to turn. I would have moved on by then, and what would I be looking out onto in the October mornings? The harsh squawking of a magpie sounded, then another responded, and another, and instantly there was a cacophony of noise, not only the birds' calls, but the clattering from their wings as they flapped about in the ash trees nearby. Looking out of the window as I prepared for the day, I could see the shiny black and white birds bouncing from branch to branch and flapping their wings. Suddenly I saw a large black bird fly out from the branches, and the magpies flew after it – I realised that a crow had ventured into their territory, and they were evicting it as a community. The sociability of these birds, and others, was interesting for me to watch. There were links to my old Community there, how they protected their own, and segregated themselves from other groups of birds. I now seemed to belong to a much more varied Community, one that welcomed others, like the crowds of little birds, finches and tits, that gathered around the hanging bird feeders in the trees closer to the staff room.

One of these feeders had squirrel-proofing as part of its manufacture, and as the squirrels descended the hanging wire, onto the roof of the container, it would reach downwards to the peanuts behind the wires, only to be frustrated by the metal cylinder it was forced to grip to reach this easy nutrition slid slowly down to conceal the food from all attempts to graze. The frustrated squirrel then dropped to the floor, only to see the cylinder bounce back upwards to the clear area beneath the roof, thus exposing the food to the birds who had retreated from the squirrel. These little creatures were persistent, and several attempts were made, until the realisation that in this case, humans had outfoxed them, and the hungry animal leapt off to another, easier target. My own breakfast would be easier to come by, I wouldn't need to seize it from smaller, hungrier, beings, merely meet Delma at the counter to select my porridge / pancakes / pastries and coffee. Once I had feasted, I set off to Elizabeth's office, for the meeting with my new employers. There were preparatory discussions to have, and I wanted to be sure I didn't forget anything. The excitement of my new life was mounting, and I wanted to be sure I could let them see that I would be doing a good job. I had researched the city I would be living in and had a few things I wanted to ask about the availability of education for me as I wanted to continue with the learning I had begun. My interest in science was increasing, and I was hoping to find out more about the genetics of inbreeding. More and more questions were raising themselves in my mind.

Elizabeth was sitting in her office, behind her desk and indicated that I should sit opposite her, as I did so, she asked me for my thoughts on what I had read about the family. I knew that there were three children, all at school, ranging in age from 7 to 13. I knew that the parents were highly educated, something that was completely alien to the Community, and I was keen to find out more about their experience and jobs. I wanted to know what sort of school the children went to, what their interests were and how much involvement I would have with them. Elizabeth helped me to compile a list of points of discussion, and questions for which I would need answers, and then an alert sounded on her laptop.

'Oooh, five minutes to go Mary, shall we both sit that side? If you want me to leave at any stage, I can do that.' She moved around the desk, and we sat in the armchairs by the coffee table. Moving the laptop so that we could both fit in the screen, with a discreet background of plants and a landscape painting rather than the rather busy noticeboard with attached timetables and lists which would have been the not-very-professional alternative had we both sat behind the desk; we sat down as the 'trying to connect' alert sounded, and then Elizabeth clicked on the Accept button.

'Hello!' we all said at exactly the same moment. And so, the meeting began with us all laughing. In the corner of Elizabeth's laptop was a small image of Elizabeth and I, the main part of the screen was showing a middle-aged couple sitting on a sofa, with two girls and a boy sitting beside them and in front of them. The girls seemed to be the oldest and the youngest, with their brother in between. Introductions began, and I saw that I would be looking after Sophia, aged 13, Benjamin, 11 and Isabella, 7. Their parents, Michael and Grace, worked as research academics in the university, Michael was a Professor of Chemistry and Grace an Archaeologist, they both worked full time and had had a nanny to look after their children for the last few years, but she was leaving at the end of term to work for a couple who were expecting their first baby at the beginning of August - and I would be undertaking that role, renamed as a housekeeper, as the children considered themselves too grown up to have a nanny!

The conversation lasted almost an hour and ended with them taking their laptop up to the bedroom which would be mine, their nanny was in there, and she laughed as Isabella rushed in and hugged her. The room was not enormous, but had space for a bed, an armchair and a big desk too. It was obviously comfortable, and I was wished good luck by their nanny as Michael and Grace left the room and took the laptop back downstairs. They took the child free moment to confirm my rate of pay and assured me that I would have the use of a car whilst I was in their employ, and that all my living costs would be met by them. My pay would need to cover any out of house spending, and they would be able to arrange for me to use the university libraries, museums and to attend any lectures I chose, I would just need to make sure I arranged the times with Grace beforehand. This all seemed very generous, their home was a mixture of good quality and chaos, the children appeared to be lively but well-behaved and I was excited to start my job with them. They closed the conversation by saying that they would let me have their full contact details and that I should let them know on which train I would arrive, and they would meet me at the station. Also, I was to get in touch at any stage, with any questions.

'So, that went well', Elizabeth switched off the laptop, looked at me and smiled. I smiled back. I couldn't believe it – it seemed too good to be true.

'Don't think like that, Mary, why shouldn't things go well for you?'

Part 3 Big Changes

Reconnecting

The end of term approached, and I was excited to see the arrangements for various events marking the end of the school term, and the year, appear on various noticeboards. The last day of term was to be a day of festivities – sports, achievements and farewells were to be celebrated, and all parents and family members were invited to attend. Catering would be busy, and Delma had indicated that menu planning had begun well in advance. There would be the usual school breakfast, then the visitors would arrive from 9.30am. A constant supply of refreshments would be available, a buffet lunch for everyone and finally an afternoon tea would indicate that the day was over, and the pupils could leave with their parents. Sports would take place in the morning with speeches and awards after lunch. The days leading up to that day would include a lot of sorting, packing and cleaning. Other staff members said that there would be a staff meal in the refectory at about 7pm, when we would all be offered that otherwise prohibited drink – alcoholic wine! The pupils would all be gone by then, and we would therefore be allowed to enjoy a glass or two with our meal. Apparently, the meal would mainly be leftovers from the day, but I understood that the atmosphere was usually great and the following day we would start our own packing. The cleaning team would be asked to give the buildings a final clean, then the big lock up would begin. An events company would use the school for training courses and conferences during the summer holidays, and I would have the option to work for them if I wanted to. I hadn't received anything formal about that, so I parked that thought and focussed on the fast-approaching end of term. My driving test was confirmed for the last week of term, and I had several lessons a week booked. I was determined to pass; my driving teacher had been very positive about my driving skills and had taken care to expose me to as many different sets of conditions as possible. I knew how to pull over for emergency vehicles, my roundabout priorities were amazing, and I had even practiced a 'scissors junction'. We had had to drive some way to find that, but it was worth it. What a strange piece of highway planning that was! I was trying to arrange for some motorway practice, which would help me to be fully confident on all roads, but I would have to wait until I had passed my test for that - I had booked in two sessions for after my test, if I failed my test, I would cancel both. My teacher was very understanding, for which I was grateful.

The next couple of weeks flew by and all too soon the final week of term was just around the corner. The cleaning schedule was up to date, the sports facilities were tidy and clean, and the science department was spotless. There was a chance that the parents visiting on the last day would want to look around, and they were encouraged to do so. All hazardous substances were securely locked away, and the wall displays were up to date. I was looking forward to seeing the school grounds full of families, I understood that there was a sort of funfair booked for those who would like to take part too. The sports would be held on the athletics ground, the sports pitches, in the tennis courts and in the pool, some in the gymnasium too, and the awards would be made at the afternoon speeches. These would be held in an enormous tent (Sally had told me it was really called a marquee) which was to be pitched in front of the main building. Hundreds of chairs had been hired, a small stage had been erected at one end of the marquee, where winners would present themselves to receive their certificates. All of this was so unusual for me to see, let alone be amongst, I was getting used to having many new experiences, but I was still surprised by the amount of fun and celebrating that went on in the world.

In the Community, there were very few celebrations, the main one we would all have to attend was the nomination of a Senior Man. He would be selected by other men in the Community and would likely be someone with a significant business (and therefore wealth), or perhaps who had legal contacts in the Outside world. One of the rules by which we lived was that we could not work in any role where we would need a University degree as to attending University, was forbidden given that we would come into too much contact with Outsiders. The more contact Community members had with Outsiders, the more likely they would be to see the attractions and many positives of the Outside world. As Community members were so tightly enmeshed financially, should they start to leave this would put the Community finances at risk. It was known that the Great Authority was a very wealthy man and I began to wonder about the finances of the Community. Was there a stream of finance to this person? It was understandable that he would want the Community members to remain and to continue the funding of his position, that Community members leaving could lead to the eventual dissolution of the Community and thus the downfall of the Great Leader were uncomfortable thoughts.

I had learned, whilst in the Community, that terrible things would happen to me, I would be injured (physically or spiritually) by evil people, I would be raped by a drunken man, thus eliminating my chances of marriage, I would become hooked on drugs and earn the disapproval of my Community and, of course, God. At that stage I wanted my Community to approve of me and had seen the isolation techniques employed on those who transgressed. I knew that some of the Senior Men had contacts in the Outside world who were happy to work for the Community, and relationships with people such as lawyers were difficult to keep and maintain.

One of the ways in which the Community men were encouraged to stay obedient to the Community rules was through fear. Fear of total financial ruination if they left or tried to leave. I remembered that Libby's family had left their Community suddenly, leaving their house and other property, they had probably changed their names too, as it was not unknown for a private prosecution to be taken out against ex-members of the Community. Thus, incurring legal costs, which would be met by the Community funds on one side, but only by the pocket of the leaver on the other. Legal fees can add up very quickly, and soon bankrupt the leaver, thus piling on the pain and humiliation. This example would be communicated to the rest of the Community, and so discourage any opposition to the limitations imposed on the hard-pressed families. This would also encourage the Community parents to keep a tight rein on their children, teenagers were kept away from the local social scenes, and filled with fear about terrible consequences should they stray far from their parents.

As I polished and scrubbed in advance of the school's celebrations, I pondered the election of these Senior Men. The process wasn't at all what I knew now was an election, it was merely presented as such. The man in question was called to the main floor of the meeting room and announced as a nomination. Then all the other men were asked to vote. 'Those in favour…' was the cue for all men to hold up their left hand. 'Those against…' the cue for stillness and silence. The 'motion' was announced as carried, and the new man welcomed to the main bench. Women were not allowed to vote, and the idea of voting 'against' was technically 'allowed' but the actual process was understood to be Never Going To Happen. During the weeks that I had spent at Hornbeam House I had seen elections for Form Captains and the democratic process had been explained to me, and I had asked Elizabeth about women voting. She had explained the whole history of women's place in the Outside world and recommended a film to me. I had never seen a film before, so she had arranged for me to watch one on her laptop. I was transfixed by the film, the conditions that some women had lived in had shocked me, although their daily duties and routines were not dissimilar to the ones that my mother followed, in fact, all married women in the Community would spend their time cleaning and cooking. Elizabeth had been surprised when I commented as such, and that had led to quite an interesting discussion afterwards. I had told her some of my history, and she had looked shocked by some of what I had said but agreed that my decision to leave was the best thing for me. We had also spoken of my sisters, and I had mentioned the sister who appeared to live in the local town. Elizabeth had asked if I would like to try to visit her and had offered to go with me.

I wasn't sure if this would be a good thing, so said that I would think about it. I really wanted to see my sister, she hadn't looked well, and I was worried. I knew that she would have little contact with our parents and may not have had a welcome to her new husband's family. I remembered that all the times that I had seen her, I hadn't really known what to do. I wanted to approach her but couldn't work out how. I decided that if Elizabeth would come with me, it would be a good solution.

I asked Elizabeth if we could go out during one of her free sessions. The habits of a Community wife would be to go to the shops or market last thing in the evening, to get the cheaper food, and the mornings should be spent clearing after breakfast and cleaning before preparing the evening meal from yesterday's cheap shopping. Yellow sticker items and about-to-go-mouldy vegetables were the staple ingredients. Desserts would be merely home-grown fruit in season.

Buying cakes, biscuits and anything sugary for non-essential eating was frowned upon, and a wife could find herself the subject of ridicule if she tried to indulge herself or, indeed, treat her children. It almost felt as if the walls had eyes, nothing would remain a secret. I thought earlyish in the morning would be a good time to call in on the house that I had seen her going into during my driving lesson. Elizabeth and I discussed it and we decided to go and park nearby before walking to the house's driveway. If the car was there, she would knock on the door with a fictitious request for help. She would have a large plastic bottle with her and would ask for water for her car's radiator as it had broken down. This would generate the need for some sort of dialogue, and at least allow her to see through the door. If the car wasn't there, we would both approach, although Elizabeth would stand aside to allow me to speak to my sister. There was one day during the last week of term where the timings would work for this to happen, and we set off shortly after the school day started. Parking in the side street, we approached the house on the corner. There wasn't a car on the drive, so we both walked up to the white front door. I could see that there were thick net curtains hung in the front windows, this was usual practice, to prevent Outsiders from looking in through the windows. The house was a detached one, although smaller than the one I had grown up in; there was one window on the ground floor, and two windows above, which indicated that it may be a two- or possibly three-bedroomed house. The driveway was enclosed on either side by high yew hedges, and the ground was tarmacked where the car would stand.

There was a strip of mown grass about two meters wide leading up to the front window, and the tarmac extended right up to the house, and along the front of it. This would allow my sister to clean the windows without having to stand on the grass, or the mud of a flower bed. The house didn't have a porch, the door opened straight onto the garden, and I could see that the area had recently been swept. My sister was doing the required tasks to prevent Outsiders having a point to make and giving no cause for people to approach her front door. The Community resisted all interaction with Outsiders, and for this reason many children didn't have regular check-ups with a doctor or a dentist. It wasn't unusual for a Community family to move away from their home town without leaving advice of change of address with the hospital where their baby had been born. It was relatively easy to live under the radar if minimum contact was made with all authorities. The main focus was to keep the Community private from the rest of the world.

Elizabeth stood to the right of the front door, well away from the front window where she wouldn't be visible to anyone at the door, or to someone in the front room. I lifted my hand and knocked on the door. There was neither a door knocker nor a doorbell, so I rapped with my knuckles on the wooden door. This was also to put random callers off, making it more difficult to attract attention, callers would be more likely to think they couldn't be heard and would leave. I knocked again, I could hear slight noises indoors, a sound like a door closing. I knocked once more, and the door slowly opened a little way. The pale face of my sister appeared in the narrow space she had allowed when holding the door. The light of recognition showed in her eyes, swiftly followed by fear.

'What are you doing here?' she whispered, and I could see the paleness of her face now extended to her lips. She looked very unwell and had black shadows under her eyes. She had been quite a smiley girl when I had lived with her, very quiet and not prone to chatter, unlike our blonde sister, but it looked as if her face hadn't smiled for a long while.

'I wanted to see how you are.' I said quickly, then 'How are you?'

'I'm all right,' she said, 'I must go now.'

The door began to close.

'Please don't,' I spoke quietly, looking her in the eye, 'I want to talk to you. Who is your husband? Are you feeling quite well? Can we talk for a minute?' The door stopped closing and her voice came from behind it.

'Not at the moment, I must go now. Goodbye.'

I put my hand on the door and spoke again. 'Please. Please don't go. Just for a minute…' The door stayed ajar, and she looked through the tiny crack again. I could only see one eye, expressionless and dry.

'Why do you want to know? You left us. You have done bad things.'

'I haven't,' I said quickly. 'I really haven't, it's a good world to live in, I have met lots of lovely people who have shown me great kindness. Nothing bad has happened. Please open the door. I miss you and I want to spend time with you.' She looked at me for a long moment. Then the door opened a little wider.

'All right,' she said. 'We can talk for just a minute.' I sighed a little shakily, I was very relieved. I repeated my question that I had asked a moment ago. 'Who is your husband?'

'He is Joshua Readings. He is not unkind to me; we have been married for almost seven weeks. He will be home for food at midday, I must make it for him.' She paused, and I understood her meaning. If there was anything to show a change to her routine, she would be closely questioned by him. I had heard of the Readings family, that was the thing with the Community, everyone knew everyone else. I knew that the family owned a wholesaler's business, supplying protective clothing and bedding to residential care homes. The laundering of the bedding was carried out by another Community business, that business also supported several local hospitals with their bedlinen too.

'I understand, I just want to make sure you are well, you look so pale…'

'I'm all right, I just feel very tired.'

'What are you eating?' I asked her.

'Soup and bread at midday.'

'What about tonight?'

'It's meeting tonight, I won't be needing anything. Joshua will take us to his parents after meeting.'

'Won't you eat there?'

'No, well, he will, but his mother says I am failing as I am not pregnant yet. So, I have to be in the kitchen.'

I knew that that meant she would be cleaning and tidying whilst the others ate. I also knew that a not-pregnant newly married woman would be held accountable for the situation. Women grew the baby, so any problems connected to that were squarely the fault of the woman. I had heard my brothers talking before I had left – they had been very critical of my older sister, whose husband had been killed. That she hadn't been pregnant was a source of disgrace, and it was possible that my other sister would have problems making a marriage now, as two of her sisters were showing difficulties in getting a baby. That my sister had only been married seven weeks was not considered. All women were expected to become pregnant straightaway. I was upset to hear that her husband's mother wouldn't allow her to eat with the rest of the family.

The men ate first in any case, with the women eating afterwards. That she looked so pale continued to be a problem for me. I didn't know what to do.

'Can we meet and talk again soon?' I asked her.

She paused and looked directly in my eyes. A long pause. 'All right' she said 'When?'

'Next week. On Tuesday morning. Shall I come here?'

She nodded and closed the door.

Testing times

I turned and walked away. Elizabeth hastened after me. We got to the end of the short driveway and turned back the way we had come, back towards the car. We walked quickly, without running, Elizabeth unlocked the car as we approached and we got in quickly, driving away at the next break in traffic. As we drove away from the town centre, through the suburbs towards the open spaces that surrounded Hornbeam House, Elizabeth was quiet, until we stopped at a set of traffic lights.

'How do you feel, having met your sister, Mary?'

'I'm glad she spoke to me, but I'm a bit concerned about her. She looks so pale.'

'Does she see a doctor. Mary?'

'I wouldn't think so, she would prefer to stay away from a hospital or a doctor.'

'I think it would be wise for her to see a doctor, Mary, if you think that she doesn't look well. It doesn't sound as if she is very well supported, and she sounds quite weak, is that how she usually speaks?'

'No, she usually sounds more like me... I'm quite worried, her lips were pale as well as the rest of her face. That's not good, is it?'

'No, not really. What do you want to do?'

'I will go to see her on Tuesday, and I'll take some food. I know what she is likely to accept, and if I don't try to eat with her, she should be happy to eat it. What do you think might be wrong with her?'

'I don't really know, but I think she should get her iron levels checked by a blood test. You could maybe persuade her to go with you to the emergency room in the hospital, or to a walk-in centre.'

'I don't know if she would go, the Community doesn't like to attract attention.'

'But she does need to get checked, she could be seriously unwell.'

'Right, I'll encourage her to go with me.'

When we got back to the school, I went off to the library and tried to find out what such a pale appearance could mean. I was very worried by some of the possibilities, and considered what I should do as I continued with my cleaning that afternoon. The sports' day on the last day of term was only a couple of days away now, and I was very keen to see how a day of celebration would be. I could see that strings of small triangular flags in different colours were being looped around the playing fields, the overall length could be several miles, and they really made the competition areas look cheerful. Tables were being set up under awnings, and I knew that these were refreshment areas. Delma had told me that there would be fruit punch served, and other chilled drinks. Additionally, there would be biscuits, cookies and other snacks which would keep all the pupils and guests satisfied until it was time for afternoon tea. I could also see some huge trailers being parked in each area and these turned out to be lavatory trucks! There were several toilet cubicles in each truck, along with wash basins, baby-changing facilities and the usual mirrors and suchlike that would be expected in any washroom. There was a separate cubicle at the rear of the truck that would be lowered to ground level on the day to allow access for disabled people. It seemed that everything had been considered and it would be a lovely way to end a term of hard work by teachers and pupils.

I went to bed tired that evening, and still my thoughts were dominated by my sister's pale face. After an uncomfortable night, not just because of the summer temperatures, and some worrying dreams involving the pale, haunting image of my sister drifting around the school grounds like a ghost, wistfully watching families enjoying themselves as they ate the offerings from the tables under the bunting-bedecked awnings, I woke with the conviction that I should go to see her much sooner than next Tuesday. Today was the day of my driving test, and my teacher would call for me at the end of the drive at 9.30am. I would have an hour's lesson before she would take me to the driving test centre where I would change my passenger from my teacher to my examiner and I would then drive according to their instructions for the next forty minutes or so. I would then be guided back to the test centre to pick up my teacher, and the examiner would tell me whether I had passed or failed. I was, of course, hoping beyond all hope that I would pass the test and I would then be able to fulfil my duties with my employer family later during the summer. I decided that I would ask the driving teacher to drop me off at my sister's house after my test and I would see how she was, my dream was only a dream, but I was convinced that I should just check on her. Walking briskly down the road to meet my driving teacher, I held in my hand a bag with some sandwiches and some slices of fruit cake. I was hoping that my sister would eat these and give me the peace of mind that she was doing a bit better. I ran the last fifty yards or so as I could see my driving teacher waiting at the gateway for me. This was it; my test would be very soon. During my lesson, I performed each manoeuvre at least once, approached every single junction type that I could and reminded myself of the different pedestrian crossings I may come across.

Then we pulled up in front of the test centre and a tall man with a light brown moustache approached the car. He got into the recently vacated passenger seat and introduced himself as Zac, as he offered his hand for me to shake. I handed him my learner's licence and he took it to check that the details matched his paperwork. Thus reassured, he asked me to start the car and to drive to the end of the road, then to turn left at the junction. This was a relaxed start to the session as Zac directed me around the town, asking me to 'park over there', 'turn right at the next junction', 'take the third exit at the roundabout ahead' and finally to 'stop the vehicle by means of the brakes when I clap my hands'. As we returned to the test centre, we drove along one of the main roads into the town, a type of road that I now knew was called an arterial road. Suddenly, someone stepped off the kerb and walked across the road. I pressed the brake pedal hard and the car stopped suddenly. The examiner clutched his clipboard and there was a thud as his mobile phone slid off the seat into the footwell. The person, who I could now see was a man, raised his hand in apology and disappeared down a side street. I sat there with my hands shaking slightly.

'Thank you, please continue when you are ready.' Zac breathed evenly, but I took a deep breath as I started the routine of setting off, looking in my mirror and checking that the correct gear was selected. No traffic was behind me, no errant pedestrians in front of me and so we continued on our way to the Test Centre. Upon arrival, I parked the car 'using forward and reverse gears', switched off the engine and sat listening to my heartbeat slow down to its usual pace. There was some rustling from my passenger and a grunt as he bent down to retrieve his phone which he was trying not to tread upon.

'Well, I am pleased to say that you have passed the test for safe driving and would ask that you submit this approval to the licensing authority as soon as you can. They will send you a full licence and I offer the authority's congratulations on the outcome of the test.' He paused, then said, 'and by the way. That emergency stop on the way back was really good - my personal congratulations on that!'

I thanked him and took the papers he held out to me resolving to send them off straightaway. He got out of the car, and my teacher returned – I passed on the good news, gratefully receiving congratulations. I said that I would like to send off for the licence straightaway and we went to the local post office to do so. Sending the licence away with the signed confirmation forms of my success felt good, and I looked forward to receiving the new licence soon. I had had to use Libby's address as I would shortly be moving on from the school, and I knew that Libby would send it on to me wherever I was. Libby and I would be friends forever, I was certain of that. We had had similar starts in life, and with her help I had made a good start on my new life. Once back in the car, we drove back towards the school, and I asked if I could be dropped off at my sister's house. Remembering to collect the bag of food from the back seat, I got out around the corner from my sister's house, thanking for my lift and all the time taken for my driving lessons and test I then turned around and walked quickly back up the road to the house I had visited so recently. It was approaching lunchtime, and I knew that she would be preparing the midday meal for Joshua. He would return home for his lunch and so I would need to be careful.

I approached the front door and knocked on the sun-warmed wood with my knuckles. Again, I knocked. Still no response. This time I thumped on the door with my fist and eventually I heard some fumbling at the door. It took almost a minute for my sister to open the door. It opened very slowly, and my sister's face appeared, looking paler than ever. I was determined, in that second, to take her to hospital.

'Rachel, you look quite unwell, I must take you to a doctor.'

'No,' she whispered, 'I can't. I can't…'

'I'll come with you,' I said, 'we'll go now.' I took her hand, it felt so fragile. Like a handful of feathers, the skin looked so thin, the bones were quite prominent, and the veins stood proud, giving her hand a very elderly appearance. Her wrist bones looked enormous. I asked her where her house key was, she shook her head.

'Joshua…' I understood. He had the key with him. I looked at my phone, selecting the number for the local taxi company. The school sometimes used taxis if the pupils needed to be taken to the train during school hours, so I had the number ready.

'Hello? Yes, I'd like a taxi please. Number 17, New Brighton Road. Immediately, please. Yes, Thank you. Oh, for two adults. Great. We'll look out for him.'

Rachel was by now swaying slightly. I took her back inside and sat her down on the stairs. The house was typically sparsely furnished, and I looked into the kitchen. I could see my sister's pathetic attempts to prepare food for her husband. Some roughly chopped vegetables were in a colander, and a saucepan of steaming water stood ready to accept its load of soup ingredients. I turned off the hob and closed the kitchen door behind me. Returning to the stairs where Rachel sat, leaning her head against the wall, I spoke to her.

'Come on Rachel, I can hear the taxi…'

She sat up and looked at me, her eyes were quite sunken and shadowed.

'We must go, Rachel. We need to get you checked. Do you want to leave a note for Joshua?'

She nodded and jumped as the taxi sounded its horn from the driveway. I wrote a quick note to Joshua, just saying 'had to go out, I'll be back later. Rachel.' I knew he wouldn't be happy, but I had to get Rachel to the hospital. I helped Rachel up and led her into the driveway. Checking I had my bag containing the food, and my phone, I then pulled the door closed behind me. We got into the taxi, in the back seat, and I asked the driver who was sitting tapping his fingers on the steering wheel to take us to the nearest hospital with an emergency room. He looked at me through his rear-view mirror.

'Sure, will do. Um, is everything all right?'

Rachel was leaning against me, and her eyes were closed. I hadn't touched her for years, since she was about three years old, it felt strange, but I could see that she wasn't in a good way. The taxi drove quickly to the hospital, using the bus/taxi lanes to hasten our arrival. Rachel slumped further against me. She was now saying nothing and didn't answer when I spoke to her. The driver paused at a set of traffic lights and looked at me again.

'You all right back there? How's your friend?'

'I don't know, I'm a bit worried. Are we nearly there?'

'Two minutes, love. Don't worry...'

A couple of ambulances shot past us with their lights flashing and sirens shrieking, I knew we must be almost there. He swung the car down the driveway to the main Emergency entrance and I unclipped our seat belts. Rachel was still slumped, and I was really worried now. The driver stopped the car and got out. He opened my door and looked at Rachel. 'She doesn't look too good, can I help?'

'Yes, please. I don't know where we go now, what shall I do?' I had tears running down my face now. I was so worried. The driver went round to the other door and opened it. He reached in and carefully picked up Rachel.

'Wow, there's nothing to her...' He carried her as if she was a small child, her head lolled sideways, and I could see that her headband was slightly askew, and her long black hair looked dull and straggly. I closed the taxi doors and ran after him, still clutching the bag containing the food. I followed the man who was now carrying Rachel to the reception desk. I caught up with him as the receptionist stood up and directed him to a doorway on the left. He hastened through there and I ran after him.

'She's my sister...' I tried to sidestep round a lady wearing what looked like some rather featureless blue pyjamas who was reaching out to me.

'We need to book her in, can you come over here?'

The taxi driver had placed Rachel on a plastic bench, a sort of mattress on legs with wheels, and was taking his leave.

'I haven't paid you,' I said as I was being drawn away.

He shook his head and waved, 'No worries love, deal with what you have to deal with. I hope she's better soon.' He walked back down the corridor and disappeared through the swing doors.

The lady in pyjamas had introduced herself as a senior nurse and was asking for details. All I could do was offer her Rachel's name and explain that I was her sister. I was asked to sit in a different room and told that they would come to see me soon. I sat for a while, wondering what to do, then decided that I would see what was happening. I left the room and found my way back to the trolley that had Rachel on it, there were several people around her and I could hear some of what they were saying.

'Very obvious chronic anaemia'

'test for pregnancy'

'…observations…'

'…severely underweight…'

'…admission immediately…'

'…more information…'

'Next of Kin…'

I felt panic start to rise in my chest, and I turned and walked rapidly through the same swing doors as the taxi driver. I needed time to think.

Worries

I walked out of the hospital building, into the grounds. I was still holding my bag containing the food I had intended to take to Rachel and so I went to an area of the grounds where some benches were set and I sat on one; a rather worn wooden bench with a small brass plate set in the back stating the grateful thanks from the family of Doris, who had loved life and would never be forgotten. I considered the wording. Had Rachel loved life? Had I? I had never really considered this before – I had grown up simply accepting that I was alive and was here to make things easier for my parents until I was granted a family of my own and then I would have several children and continue the process of encouraging the girls to stay quiet, acquiescent and obedient, whilst the boys would be encouraged to do the same until they were of an age when they would start to consider how they would support a family. I would have expected a lot of guidance from the Community for this, and any autonomous thoughts or behaviour on my part would not have been considered appropriate. Enjoying life hadn't ever been considered – and I thought about Rachel, lying on that trolley, more like a gurney than anything else, with no-one she knew around her, but plenty of strangers. I decided that she should not be alone, she should get better and get out of hospital, then start to enjoy life in the way that I was. She was a year older than I was and deserved so much more than she had. A grey existence, in the shadow of a grey man who didn't know that there was a life of enjoyment to be had. Who had never known that it was safe to live in the proximity of those who weren't in the Community.

I hadn't yet worked out what the pull of the Community was, why my parents were so willing to comply with so many restrictions on their lives and seemed so blind to all those enjoyable events around them. My own eyes had started to open a few years earlier, because of my teacher, but my parents MUST have had interactions with Outsiders, I wondered why they hadn't thought any more about those. I reflected for a minute as I ate the slice of fruit cake from the school pantry and realised that I hadn't mentioned my thoughts to anyone about what I had heard my teacher say to me, I had learned to keep my thoughts to myself. So, I hadn't been corrected, although I knew that there had been consequences for listening to her. Rachel, and as many others as I could manage, should know about the safety of the outside – yes, bad things could happen, but some of the things that happened within the Community were bad too. All of them should be allowed to choose, and only knowing that the Outside was 'the way to Hell' was not enough information to make an informed decision. Living under a cloud of fear wasn't a healthy way to live. My thoughts turned to my other sisters; I was still wondering about my blonde sister having a different appearance from the rest of us, and now I was beginning to have some very unhappy thoughts about my poor sister. Maybe help for her would have made her life a considerably different existence.

 I had only been in the hospital for a few minutes, but I had seen so many people, with 'things wrong with them' and they had been treated exactly the same as others around them with 'nothing wrong with them', whereas my poor sister had always been treated as if she had no thoughts of her own. I could see that although I had changed a lot since leaving the Community, I would need to adopt some more new ways of thinking. This could well be overwhelming for Rachel, and others within the Community, so I would have to think carefully about what to do. I should ask Libby and maybe Elizabeth for advice. It was too much for me to handle alone. I finished the cake and sat in the sunshine for a few minutes. I knew that I had to return to Rachel and see how she was. I thought that if I took her back home, I would make sure we could stay in touch and we could build our relationship until she could see how happy I was and maybe she would consider leaving the Community. She would have to keep our interaction a secret from her husband, but of course she would be so much happier. I dropped the cake wrapper into a nearby waste bin and, picking up my bag, I walked back into the hospital.

Back through the swing doors where I had left Rachel, and saw the same staff clustered around the trolley. More talking was going on, and then one person stepped away and I could see that the person on the bed was now an elderly gentleman. Beside his head was an elderly lady and she was holding his hand. I stood still and felt my mouth go dry. I caught hold of the lady who had left the group as she walked past me - she turned and looked at me.

'Yes?'

'Where has Rachel gone? She was here a few minutes ago?'

'Oh, she's been transferred. Let me find someone who can help us...'

I was suddenly alone. Where had Rachel gone...? I looked around, feeling slightly panicky. What could I do? After a couple of minutes, a man in the apparent uniform of plain blue pyjamas pushed his way through another set of swing doors and walked towards me.

'Rachel's sister? Can you follow me please?'

He led me through to the same room that I had left a while earlier.

'Please, sit down. We must have a chat. Rachel has been taken through to the High Dependency Room, it's quite early to be certain as we will have to test further, but it does seem that Rachel has a problem with her blood. We don't know how it may affect her just yet, but please understand that she is seriously ill. We haven't got any records for her, so we will need to ask a few more questions.' He looked at me and was silent for a while. Then he spoke more gently, 'What can you tell me about Rachel please?'

'What do you need to know?' I countered, with the almost instinctive concern about divulging Community information to any authority.

He sighed, 'we really need to know anything you can tell us about her health. I know that you are her sister, do you have living parents?'

I nodded.

'I really need to speak to her next of kin, I should speak to one of her parents. Could you let us know their contact details please?'

'Wouldn't her next of kin be her husband?'

'She's married??! How old is she please?'

'She's twenty. She's been married only a few weeks.'

'Right, we need to get in touch with her husband then. Do you have a number for him?'

I shook my head. 'I can go and get him?'

He looked at me again, thoughtfully. 'Is there a reason you don't have a number for him? It does sound a bit unusual, and we need to get help for Rachel as soon as we can. We wondered if she has any particular religious beliefs, her clothing is quite distinctive and one of our members of staff pointed out that we may need to check any religious convictions.'

I hesitated, the Outside world had really only helped me, and Rachel did need a lot of help. 'Yes, she is part of a Community, and so is her husband. She hasn't had any medical help so far in her life, so that's why you don't have any information about her. I left the Community a couple of months ago, so I haven't met her husband, but I do know where he lives.'

'Right, we need to get permission from him as a Next of Kin, so we need him here. Do you have a car?'

'No, I came by taxi.'

'What is his address please?'

I told him their address and he said that he would arrange for him to be picked up. I thought he meant by a member of staff, so I was rather surprised when, about fifteen minutes later I saw Joshua being brought into the waiting room. He was accompanied by two policemen, one of whom nodded at me and sat down by the door, and Joshua, looking bewildered and rather angry, sat down opposite the door. This little room was getting rather crowded now, there were about six chairs, a small coffee table which held a half empty box of tissues and a large plastic cube full of water on top of a stand which could dispense water into a small cardboard cup when a button was pressed. As the cup was removed and the button released, a bubble of air fought its way through the water, erupting on the surface with a muffled 'bloop' sound. With three people in there, there was quite a crowd, and then the second policeman and the same doctor who had recently spoken to me entered and they both sat down around the coffee table. The doctor was holding some paperwork which he began to spread out on the table.

'Thank you for coming in Mr Readings, I'm sorry we meet like th-'

'I would really like to know what is happening! I came home from work for lunch to find no food, no wife and then a policeman knocks on the door and brings me here. I have done nothing illegal, why am I being treated like a criminal? I really mus-' Joshua interrupted the doctor with a stream of indignation, but stopped as the doctor raised one hand saying, quite firmly.

'Mr Readings, Sir, Please!'

Joshua fell silent but grew quite red in the face.

'We do have to move fairly quickly here; Rachel is quite unwell and needs treatment immediately. I have a consent form here; she had had an emergency scan already and we have performed initial checks on her blood. We cannot be certain of the cause yet, but she has very low iron levels, we may need to give her a blood transfusion in due course, our investigations will show more soon. She has not been conscious since she arrived, and I would like you, Mr Readings to sign these forms as her next of kin, to allow us to undertake further steps necessary to help her.' He pushed the forms over to Joshua and offered a pen.

'I really cannot see why I should...'

The doctor interrupted him again, 'Sir, we really can't waste time, to give Rachel a chance we need to proceed.'

'Joshua, please just sign them.' I heard a voice, shrill with fear. It was mine.

Joshua turned sharply and spoke. 'How dare you address me so, who are you anyway?'

'Do you want your wife to die? Mr Readings?' The doctor was standing up by now. Joshua stood up too.

'Now gents, let's think of the young lady. Is there a reason that you cannot sign these forms sir?' One of the policemen had also stood up and was attempting to calm both men down. The doctor took a deep breath and tried once more. 'I realise that this had been a shock Mr Readings, but Rachel is very seriously ill and if we act quickly, we could save her. Any delay could be very dangerous to her. Please, won't you sign the forms?'

Joshua looked at him, still red and angry, then he looked at the policemen. One still standing up, with one hand outstretched towards the two men standing face to face, the other still sitting by the door, with one hand covering the black box clipped to the front of his bright yellow jacket, and I was reminded of the first meeting I had had with the police, all those weeks ago in Libby's house. She had subsequently explained that any policeman involved in contact with members of the public wore on their outer clothing a radio which would immediately contact the headquarters, and also a camera which would record everything in front of them, and any speech. Joshua swallowed and looked at the forms.

'Right,' he sat down, scribbled his name on the forms and sat drooping his head and fidgeting his fingers. He suddenly looked quite young and vulnerable. I thought of my brother, how would he feel in Joshua's position? The doctor picked up the papers, thanked him and saying that he would be back in due course, left the room, followed by the policeman who had remained standing up. The room was silent again, apart from the rustling of the policeman's big yellow coat and the crackling sounds for his radio. Realizing that the lunch hour would now be over at school, I started to message Elizabeth to excuse my absence. I said that I was quite well myself, but that Rachel had been taken to hospital and that I was with her.

A few minutes later my phone began to ring, and I could see that Elizabeth was the caller. Excusing myself, I left the room and answered her call a little way down the corridor. She asked if I was all right and I explained the situation. She suggested I return to school, but I should leave my telephone number with the medical staff. Now that Joshua was present it may be wisest to leave him to talk to the staff without me. She was glad to know that the police were there and said that they would be able to help Rachel. She said that she would drive down to the hospital to pick me up and would be there in about twenty-five minutes.

I went back into the hospital and looked for the doctor. I decided that the best person to look for would be the policeman who was accompanying him, and I followed the sound of the crackling radio.

'I have to go back to work now,' I said, and asked if I could leave my number with the doctor.

'I should think so', he said and looked in through a doorway. 'The sister's leaving, wants to leave her number.'

A different person came out, and took off their mask, I could see that I was talking to a lady this time, 'I'm Doctor Rowe,' she said. 'You're going to leave us your number?' Her tone rose slightly at the end of the sentence, questioningly. 'Yes please, its…' I recited the number to her, and she wrote it onto a form from a folder on the desk in front of her and read it back to me to make sure she had the information correctly.

I looked at Doctor Rowe, 'I really do need to know how she is, she's my sister.'

'Nevertheless, we can only let you know what she wants us to. If she wants us to. Would you be able to visit? She's likely to be transferred to a ward once we have finished helping her, if you telephone tomorrow, the information centre would be able to tell you which ward she is on, and then you could perhaps speak to the staff there. If they have her permission, they will be able to fill you in then.'

'What if they don't have her permission? What if she hasn't yet woken up?'

'They will be able to say whether she is awake, and whether she can be visited. They can't stop you coming to the hospital, unless there is a court order, if Rachel doesn't want you to visit, they will let you know that.' It didn't sound very satisfactory but seemed to be the only option that I had. At least they could get in touch with me, and I tapped in the hospital's number in to my phone before thanking her and starting to walk back to the main entrance. The twenty-five minutes were almost up, and Elizabeth would be here to pick me up soon. Joshua appeared out of the waiting room as I passed by, and he seized my arm quite roughly.

'Who ARE you?' He said menacingly... 'What are you doing here, how dare you interfere with Rachel's business.'

I looked him in the eye, 'It's my business too, Rachel's my sister. I love her and want her to be well. I'm sure you do too.'

The policeman had followed Joshua out of the room and put his hand onto the wrist of Joshua's hand that was holding my arm so tightly.

'I don't think that's necessary do you, Sir? Let the lady go.'

Joshua swallowed and let go of my arm. I could see from his expression that he thought it was very necessary indeed, he wasn't used to women speaking to him so assertively and that I had said I was Rachel's sister was causing him great confusion. He didn't seem to know anything about me. Maybe he thought I was an imposter, a liar. But why would I pretend to be her sister, why would I lie?

There was still rage showing in his expression; I had challenged him, made a fool of him and forced the authorities onto his household. All were unpardonable actions in the Community, but as I wasn't in the Community, he was powerless, and this was the cause of the rage. I knew, with the wisdom of an Outsider, that he had brought all this upon himself, but that he hadn't the knowledge to understand that. His understanding had been so warped by the Community that he thought that his treatment of Rachel was acceptable. I could see that he may soon be having a few uncomfortable conversations with the medical staff and police staff.

Getting into Elizabeth's car a couple of minutes later, I was feeling slightly dazed. Elizabeth, in her usual quiet way, said hello as I put on my seatbelt and sighed.

'How did you get on? What brought you to the hospital?' She guided her car out of the hospital grounds, and I told her about my visit to Rachel's house and her subsequent collapse as I took her to hospital in a taxi. Keeping Elizabeth updated with what had happened took a few minutes and we drove out of the town towards school. Finally, I stopped talking, and Elizabeth told me how wise I had been, and that I had done exactly the right thing.

Parking her car in the school car park, she switched off the engine and said, 'one thing I want to ask though, how did the driving test go?'

'Oh!' I had completely forgotten about that, 'I passed!!' She laughed delightedly and hugged me.

'Well done, you've done so well! What a day this is turning out to be!'

Celebrations

The last day of term dawned brightly, I showered and dressed quickly. It had taken me a few weeks to adjust to a frequent showering regime. At home we had only bathed on Saturdays, in advance of the main weekly meeting. We were kept so busy with school, chores and evening meetings during the week that it was impossible for us to adopt a routine similar to the one I was now enjoying. As I dried my hair with my hairdryer, another recent time-saving device which would have been considered a shameful luxury, I looked out of my bedroom window, high up on the third floor of the building. I could see the bunting fluttering between the trees, between the awnings where the refreshments would be served later. Already there were big banners being erected stating what was available at a particular stand. DRINKS. TEAS. ICE CREAM. WASHROOMS. These were repeated around the premises, more than one of each hand-sewn banner had been made, as there were several areas to be serviced. The sewing classes had been very busy preparing these, the foot-high letters had been cut out of fabric that would otherwise have been discarded, then sewn onto huge strips of cotton, rumoured to be old bedsheets which gave the banners a patchwork yet co-ordinated appearance. I knew that holes had been left in the middle of letters R, D, O and A, to reduce the likelihood of the wind catching the banner and it becoming a sail!

Members of the janitorial team were attaching white cloths to the countertops under the awnings and allowing the cloth to drape down to the ground on the front and sides of the tables, to give the appearance of tablecloths, but widely rumoured to be yet more bedsheets. I considered that a school this size, where several hundred beds were in use, would have a huge stock of bedsheets, and so these could be well-used for this purpose. I had seen the laundry area, there were huge washing machines, a drying green as well as tumble drying machines and several large ironing presses. These looked like a set of rollers where the sheets would be folded in half, fed in at one side, travel through several sets of rollers, with the two pairs at the end pressing the sheets flat with steam permeating through some tiny holes. The steaming sheet was dispensed into a kind of automated clothes horse which folded it concertina-wise as the sheet dried, and a staff member would be available to direct the neatly folded sheet to a trolley ready to be returned to the storage area. I knew the feeling of the clean, crisp sheets on my bed, and relished laundry day.

My mother had always kept our beds changed regularly and we girls had been tasked with the laundry to make this happen. No such automation for us though, we had a simple washing machine, which needed someone to be in attendance, to move the laundry from the washing drum containing soapy water to the spin dryer side, and to add the rinsing water before setting off the final spin cycle. Then the laundry would have to be removed and hung on a long rack which was winched up to the ceiling to dry. Once it was dry it was time for the ironing. We had to look well presented to avoid the criticism that would follow from the other women if it was apparent that the ironing had not been completed well. Time-saving conveniences weren't really approved of in the Community, these would indicate laziness and idleness on our part. Being able to take the time to appreciate the world's beauty had been a great pleasure to me since I had been living in Hornbeam House; I was kept pretty busy, but if I did stop to watch some birds, some rabbits or other wildlife I could take my time to appreciate them. I never grew tired of cloud-watching, seeing the clouds change shape as they moved across the sky, watching the changing colours in the clouds at sunrise or sunset. My favourite time was waking early and watching the sun rise, hearing the birds calling and seeing the sky get brighter.

Running down the stairs, I went into breakfast to fuel up for the morning. We had been encouraged to eat a little more than usual, as we would be very busy getting the final preparations done before the first parents started arriving at 10am. The teaching staff would be checking all the pupils' rooms, checking that the packing had been done and that all the bags were ready to be taken downstairs at the end of the day. Sports kits were to be worn for the morning, as most pupils would be appearing in one of the competitions, and these would be taken off and put into the main bag by lunchtime. Pupils would be expected to attend the awards and speeches in their freshly washed and ironed summer uniform, candy striped shirts in different colours, depending on the year group of the pupil, and navy trousers or skirts. The days of expecting girls to wear skirts and boys to wear trousers were long past in this school, it was up to the pupil themselves to choose. Most wore trousers, but it really was a personal choice. Community girls would, of course, have worn their long, all-concealing dresses, for fear that the appearance of their skin would call down untold harm to them both morally and physically. I could see now that the mental harm of all these fears was as bad, if not worse, than any possible physical harm.

As non-teaching staff, I was responsible for signposting and hosting when the parents arrived. This would take the form of greeting families and directing them to the relevant areas for the appropriate sports and answering any questions they may have. For now, though, I assisted the catering staff in ferrying all the glasses, plates and dishes out to the newly-sheeted tables. The food was being prepared in the kitchens now that breakfast was over, and the platters and trays would be brought out at regular intervals during the day to ensure a steady supply of food and drinks. Drinking ice would also be supplied, and a small mobile generator was brought over to one of the drinks tables to enable an ice-making machine to supply the drinks tables without the risk of melting on the walk over from the main kitchens. As platters became empty, and plates finished with, they would be discreetly collected by me and others in similar role and stacked into plastic crates placed for this purpose under the shrouded tables. Once everyone had gone to the main marquee for the awards and speeches, the dirty crockery would be taken back to the kitchens, and the afternoon teas would be brought out in time for the end of the awards. Parents and family members could then sample the remaining food and drinks whilst their offspring collected their luggage from their rooms, assisted by teaching staff, before meeting with their parents at the front of the main building and returning to the parental transport which would convey everyone, replete with Hornbeam House catering, back home for the summer. Then we would tidy up the second round of dishes and food, a buffet supper would be set out for all staff in the refectory and the janitorial team, assisted by the teaching staff, would disassemble the tables, awnings and marquees for return to storage, and the temporary tablecloths would be returned to the laundry for inclusion with the mountains of bedlinens left by the pupils.

It was set to be a busy day, but I could already feel the enjoyment in the atmosphere. This was to be my first celebration of any size and I was looking forward to it. Elizabeth had already said that I should go to either her office, or my bedroom for fifteen minutes every couple of hours, for a break from the hustle and bustle. I liked that idea, and she had given me a key for her office. As well as this and my bedroom key, I had my phone in my trousers pocket, in case I heard from the hospital. The first call of the day came through quite early in the day. I had just taken a box of champagne glasses which would be used to serve a sparkling citrus alcohol-free punch to one of the drinks tables when I heard a loud jangling noise as my phone vibrated in my pocket. I snatched it out and pressed the green button to silence the sound and to accept the call,

'Hello?'

A voice immediately answered me, asking if I was Audrey. I replied affirmatively and before I could say more, I could hear a loud siren drowning out the voice on the other end of the call. There were some other noises too, and I could hear someone asking me to hold on, a bit of banging and then quietness.

'Sorry about that, can you hear me? Are you still there? Audrey?'

'Yes, I'm here. Who is this please?'

'It's Doctor Rowe, we met yesterday, I am treating your sister, Rachel.'

'Yes, how is she?' My mouth felt dry.

'She's still very unwell, but she has responded to some of the treatment and regained consciousness. She has permitted me to ring you and has asked that you visit her when possible. She will be kept in for the next week or so, whilst we treat the causes of the problem. Can I tell her you will come in?'

'Yes, of course. I will come in tomorrow morning.'

'Marvellous, come to the main entrance and ask for Ward Twelve. I will be on duty until three o'clock. Until tomorrow then.' There was a click and the call had ended. I stood looking at the blank screen of the phone, thinking. Rachel was feeling better but had to stay in hospital. What could be wrong? I put my phone back into my pocket and turned to go back to the kitchen for the next box of glasses or plates.

'Hi Mary, how are you? Everything ok?'

I jumped, Sally was right behind me and the slightly smug smile on her face showed me that she had heard at least my side of the telephone conversation. I remembered that she had previously been fishing for personal information, so I smiled cheerfully and said that everything was fine. Walking quickly ahead of Sally, I hurried away to find Elizabeth. I wanted to ask her if I could go to visit Rachel the following morning. Luckily, I ran into Elizabeth as she was walking to the marquee with a box of booklets containing the programme for the afternoon. Hundreds of chairs were being arranged on the temporary flooring which had been fitted the previous evening. The tent, or marquee, was huge. In front of the rows and rows of chairs were rows and rows of narrow benches where the younger pupils would sit, in front of the low stage where the speeches would be made, and the awards would be presented. I caught up with her as she walked along the front row, placing one booklet on each chair.

'Hi Mary, how are you doing?'

'I'm fine thanks, could I have a quiet word please?' Just then, Sally appeared behind me.

'Hi Elizabeth, shall I do some of those? Oh, hi Mary, are you all right? You look a bit upset, what's wrong?'

'I'm fine thanks, Sally, I just need to...' suddenly Elizabeth interrupted, which wasn't her usual way.

'Oh, thank you Sally, could you put these out for me? That's so kind, thank you so much. Mary, could you do something for me? This way...' and with that, Elizabeth gave Sally a job and took me away from Sally's intrusive questioning.

'What's wrong, Mary? Sally's right about that, you DO look upset.'

I explained that I had had a phone call from the hospital saying that Rachel had asked for me to visit and I wanted to go the following morning. I wanted to go but had to check that I could be excused some of the clear-up in the morning. Elizabeth said that I could certainly go, and that she would be happy to accompany me if that would help. I paused for a minute, then accepted her offer. I didn't really know what was wrong with Rachel, and I felt I might need someone to help me understand her situation. I was getting very good at carrying out internet research about everything new that I came across, but this could take time and I felt that Elizabeth's presence would be helpful as well as reassuring. Following Elizabeth back to the main building, I returned to the kitchen to see what else I could take out to assist with the setting up. Delma directed my footsteps to the stack of boxes and trays on the big table on the left of the main kitchen door. I took the next tray of small dishes; these would be used to serve strawberries in later – I could see the staff chopping up some strawberries and putting the chopped quarters into large glass serving bowls. These smaller glass dishes would be filled from the huge bowls and sugar and whipped cream added depending on individual preference. Platters of cookies, each with its own clear domed cover would also be taken later, and these, along with plates of small savouries were being prepared by more staff. It all looked very appetising, and I knew that there would be some available to the staff later too. Once the visitors had eaten their fill, the leftovers would be set aside, and the staff would share it along with a fresh supply. That we would all sit together in the refectory once the pupils had all left, able to relax all together, helping ourselves, along with Delma and her colleagues – all sitting together, I was looking forward to that.

Results

Eventually, the races began, the Sports staff were overseeing the races and competitions and refreshments were continuously being brought over to the serving tables under their awnings. The cheering and the applause were wonderful to hear, and the clinking of spoons against the strawberry dishes was a constant backdrop to the activities. Copious quantities of the fruit punch were being dispensed to adults and children alike. Chilled water was also available, and I loved to see all the celebrations, the guests were loving everything, the pupils were having a wonderful time and the staff all seemed to be happy. There were enough staff in the right places to make the day easy for everyone. I mingled with everyone, wearing my staff lanyard I was easy to identify as a source of information, so I had plenty of interaction with many of the visitors, and the pupils. I was kept very busy all morning, but able to take my own refreshments too. The time passed very quickly, and then the announcement was made for lunch. Sandwiches, rolls, savoury pastries and patisserie cakes were all being served at the refreshment tables, people were encouraged to take a few at a time, and stood around chatting. There were benches for those who preferred to sit, and the recent dry weather meant that the more agile could sit on the grass, and that's exactly what the children and younger people did. They sat in chattering groups, with occasional squeals as a drink was spilt, but the general atmosphere was friendly and relaxed. I kept catching sight of Sally, she seemed to be fairly close to me all the time but made no attempt to speak to me. She just seemed to be there, constantly. I continued to circulate amongst the families, carrying plates for those trying to co-ordinate carrying crockery and small children, not an easy task, and I was glad to be a spare pair of hands. I still had Elizabeth's office key in my pocket and decided to go down there as soon as the speeches started, just to rest in the peaceful atmosphere. Sally's eyes being constantly on me was reminiscent of the Community, where we had been under constant scrutiny and reported on for any minor infraction. My uneasiness because of her behaviour this morning was a feeling that I had not had for a few months now, and I had got used to that freedom. I knew that she couldn't cause me any trouble, and I wasn't concerned about her motives, I knew that she was just nosey and liked to know what other people were doing. That I hadn't shared my family details with her wasn't something she could understand – we all knew everything about Sally – I wasn't too concerned about her motives, so I decided that I had no need to fear any results of her scrutiny. Sitting in Elizabeth's office a while later, I leaned back in the chair and breathed deeply, with my eyes closed I could hear all the sounds of the birds outside, and the distant muffled noises from the kitchen. Then my phone rang – I jerked back to reality and saw that it was the doctor from the hospital again.

'Hello?'

'Hello, Audrey? I'm sorry to ring again but I wonder if you could come down to us as soon as possible. Rachel has had a relapse and we would like to talk to you please.'

'Of course. I'll be there as soon as I can, I'll leave now.' As I switched off the phone, I saw that my hands were shaking slightly. I wrote a short note to Elizabeth and left it on her desk.

'Hospital called again, Rachel had a relapse, I'm going there now. Will text later. Sorry. Mary.'

I then left the office, locked the door behind me and set off to the main gates, ringing the taxi company as I did so.

'Mary? Where are you going? Is something wrong? Can I help?'

It was Sally again! she must have been standing outside the door! What was it with this lady? Why did she want to know so much about me? I felt slightly impatient as she had been my shadow for most of the day.

'No, thank you Sally. I just need to go out. I'll be back later - don't worry.'

She hurried after me. "Mary, Mary! Let me give you a lift!

'No! Thank you, Sally, that's kind but I need to leave now; see you later!' I turned my attention to the phone call which had now connected.

'Hello? A taxi from Hornbeam House as soon as possible please, yes, it's urgent. To the hospital. Thank you. I'll wait at the gateway on the main road.' I hurried down the main driveway, the taxi company had said that they would send a car immediately, and I wanted to be at the hospital with as little delay as possible. I had no idea what was meant by a relapse and wanted to be there in time to help Rachel. The huge hornbeams trees rustled their leaves gently in the breeze as I hurried down the avenue so recently the path of so many shining cars now parked to the side of the main building and across the practise pitches where hockey would take place in the winter. No squirrels were apparent this afternoon, the activity from all our visitors had probably encouraged them to wait in the branches above until peace reigned once more. On reaching the bottom of the drive I leaned against the wall, feeling the warmth of the sun on my face and the stonework on my back. I looked around, Sally was walking down the driveway towards me. Would I get no rest from her? Her nosiness was getting beyond quirky now. She arrived at the gateway at the same time as the taxi and called to me as I closed the car door. I confirmed my destination to the hospital and as the car turned round to drive back to the town, I could see her standing and watching after me. I texted a message to Elizabeth 'In taxi on way to hospital. Sally has been following me all morning. I have told her everything is fine. Back later X'. I arrived at the hospital and paid the fare; I asked the driver if he knew who had dropped me off before. From my description he thought it might have been Joe, I said I owed for that journey too so he suggested I ring back and talk to the controller who would be able to help me. I thanked him and ran into the hospital asking for Ward Twelve at the main reception. The slightly harassed-looking lady there indicated some coloured lines on the wall opposite with the instruction to follow the green line and then signs for Ward Twelve. Another thank you and I hurried along the green route.

  Upstairs along corridors, past doors that swished open silently and past doors that clunked open as a bed containing a thin figure connected to tubes and bags of liquid hanging from a framework around them was shoved out along the corridors on their way to a different source of treatment. I guessed that the greater the number of medical staff alongside, the more unwell the patient, but the care and dedication was apparent regardless of the patient's condition. Ward Twelve seemed to be quite a long way away. One bed that clunked through a set of doors had no framework attached, no tubes or bags and the figure lying still was completely covered with bedclothes. The porter pushing the bed was solemn faced and alone. Other beds had been accompanied by staff and gentle conversation. It seemed that this patient had reached the end of their life journey. I wondered what happened now. In the Community there would have been mention of this event at a meeting and, depending on the status of the person departed, praise and accolade for their life's work would be offered before solemn prayers and celebration for their arrival at their heavenly abode. Outsiders were not expected to make that journey due to their disrespectful lifestyle. The Community believed that they were the only people who were deserving of ultimate heavenly paradise due to their way of living, avoiding immoral matters and living a respectable lifestyle. I could now see that certain aspects of this supposedly respectable lifestyle were far from moral, the way that children were disciplined, for example, and the way that what I now knew were disabled people and not people with 'something wrong with them' supposedly sent as a punishment for some misdemeanour. I was more certain than ever that leaving had been the best thing for my own personal future. My only regret had been that I had had to leave my family. I was glad that I had had the chance to reconnect with Rachel but had no idea whether I would be able to continue with this relationship. Joshua didn't seem very approachable, and I would have a challenge ahead of me when interacting with him. It depended on how Rachel was, I knew that she had been happy for me to be updated but wondered what had caused this relapse. I had now arrived at the door of Ward Twelve, the sign above the double doors announced the place as High Dependency Unit, I pressed the buzzer that would bring someone to let me in. A pale blue figure became visible through the frosted glass of the door and with a click the door swung open and Dr Rowe stood before me.

Serious decisions

Doctor Rowe invited me into her office, and I drew forward the plastic chair she indicated beside a desk covered in folders and papers. I sat down and she sat at the desk.

'Thank you for coming in so quickly, Audrey, this is a really tricky time for Rachel, and I hope that you can help us to help her. We have done some initial blood work, and this indicates that Rachel is likely suffering from a type of Leukaemia. Cancer of the white blood cells. These usually help to fight infection, and Rachel has some infections which may be due to this reduced immunity, there seems to be an infection in her kidneys and there is also something wrong in her digestive system.' She paused and I sat there in shocked silence. I couldn't hear anything except her words echoing in my head. Rachel had serious problems with her blood, her kidneys and her digestive system. If she couldn't eat properly, fight infections or properly expel waste she was very seriously unwell. Doctor Rowe spoke again and there was a noticeable sound of urgency in her tone,

'I know that this is a lot to take in, Audrey. We have to act quickly and during a period of consciousness last evening, Rachel spoke during a consultation with me and two more members of staff saying that she would like for you to be involved in any decisions should she be unable to make them herself. She hasn't woken this morning and remains unconscious. She is connected to life support equipment, and we are monitoring her constantly.'

'What do we do now? She sounds to be so very ill, and I don't know enough to know whether she will get better. What is likely to happen, what can be done for her?'

'We hope to be able to help her and we will do whatever we can. We have given her some fluids overnight, which should help with the severe dehydration. Our next step is to do a full blood transfusion. Do you know her blood group?'

'I don't, sorry.' I had only recently known of such things, it seemed that living in fearful ignorance was one existence, but when something like this happened, knowledge was essential. Doctor Rowe continued to explain that replacing Rachel's dangerously infected blood with uninfected blood from a donor would help for now, and once they could help her kidneys and her bowel to function effectively again, they could focus on treating the leukaemia which in turn would help the organs to function correctly. This was likely to take more than a few weeks, Dr Rowe said that she wanted me to understand the seriousness of the situation, and that we should move swiftly to give Rachel the best chance to recover. I asked whether Rachel's husband had been involved in her care, and she said that he had been reluctant to commit to a decision, particularly about the blood transfusion. I knew that he would be conflicted about that and would likely be consulting some of the local Senior Men for advice. If Rachel received a blood transfusion, then she would be 'contaminated' by an Outsider. This would likely compromise her 'purity' and her membership of the Community may be questioned. Should she subsequently have children, they could not be guaranteed to be accepted into the Community. I knew that if I said that she could have a transfusion, she would be at risk of excommunication. Should it be known in the Community. What if they weren't told? The only one likely to come to the hospital was Joshua... did we need to tell him? Then I realised how ridiculous I was being. He knew the treatment was likely as he had been asked the day before. The hospital had not been able to get in touch with him since, which is why they were asking for my permission. Doctor Rowe explained that she had spoken to Rachel about a transfusion the evening before, but Rachel had been too weak to sign, and was unable to answer anything other than 'If Audrey or Joshua agrees, I'll do it'. I replied immediately.

'Let's do it.'

That she hadn't said 'No', told me that she wanted help, and that she had said, with witnesses, that I or Joshua could decide, made me certain. Doctor Rowe had already picked up a telephone and ordered a supply of 'Oh Neg' and was making her way to the office door.

'Would you like to see Rachel? She's through here…'

I followed, pausing at the door to the room where Rachel lay, I squirted the sterilising solution over my hands, rubbing them all over until the liquid dried and then I pushed the door open, moving forward amongst the machines beeping around me. One seemed to be representing her heartbeat as an image of a heart flashed in time with the beep, and also a zig-zaggy graph line seemed to be travelling across the lower part of the screen. Another machine was on the far side of the bed, I couldn't see what was showing on that screen and I looked at Rachel's face. Her eyes were closed, there was a tube connected to her nose, a tube in her mouth and tubes connected to her left arm, and a clip on the forefinger on her left hand. I sat on a chair on the right-hand side of the bed, Rachel's right arm was lying on the top of the bedclothes, she seemed to be wearing a thin cotton printed top with elbow-length loose sleeves. Doctor Rowe asked me to talk to Rachel and suggested I could hold her hand. I touched Rachel's hand awkwardly. We had not been brought up to hold hands, and I felt rather uncomfortable. But it was explained that sometimes unconscious patients could find comfort in the touch of someone they knew, and it could help with recovery. I sat down and took Rachel's cool, still hand in both of mine.

'Hi Rachel...' I stopped. What could I say to her? I felt strange, talking to my silent and still sister. She lay there, the surrounding machines bleeping and pinging, and I squeezed her hand gently.

'Rachel, you're quite safe, all these doctors are really working hard to help you feel better. Just rest, and you will feel better soon.'

I looked at her lying there, she seemed so peaceful. Unconcerned by all that had happened to her in the last few weeks, she appeared to be relaxed and sleeping. The machines seemed not to disturb her, and I wondered what would wake her. Then the door opened and two members of staff, wearing the hospital uniform of blue pyjamas, brought in a small trolley, containing dishes full of tubing and a pouch of maroon liquid which, judging by the staff reading the labels out loud to each other and agreeing their instructions, I deduced to be the necessary blood for Rachel's transfusion. It appeared to be blood from group O negative, which should help Rachel's situation. The pouch was hooked up to part of the framework at the head of the bed, and tubes attached it to a separate tube which had already been taped onto the back of Rachel's left hand. The staff adjusted various parts of the equipment, and when they were satisfied that the apparatus was working correctly, they asked me if I had any questions, I had nothing I wanted to ask – I was preoccupied by everything that had happened to her and was trying to work out what to do. I had allowed the transfusion to take place, and I guessed that Joshua may not be pleased about that. I was also expected back at the school to assist with the clear up, so I should return there as soon as I could. And I needed to pay the taxi company for the fare I owed them. I told Rachel that I would be back to see her tomorrow and squeezed her hand again.

I went to let Doctor Rowe know that I was leaving and to ask how long it would be before we would know whether the transfusion was working. She answered that it was difficult to say, but they would test Rachel's iron levels the following day. As I left Ward Twelve, I telephoned the taxi company and asked for a ride out to the school which could be arranged in the next fifteen minutes, so I used that waiting time to send a message to Elizabeth saying that I was returning shortly. I put my phone back in my pocket, just as the taxi arrived. I got in and confirmed that I wanted Hornbeam House; as the taxi drove out of the hospital grounds, I saw Joshua's car driving into the grounds, I guessed he was going to the car park. I was wondering what he had decided about the transfusion, when my phone bleeped, and I looked down to check the message. It was from Elizabeth, she was asking how I was getting on, so I responded saying that I was on my way back and that Rachel was unconscious but being cared for. I also took advantage of the few minutes' drive to message Libby, asking if I could return to stay for a few weeks before I went to my next job. I would be paying for my stay with her this time, and I wanted to donate to the funds of The Network, to enable her and her colleagues to help another person to make their own way, as I had been helped.

The taxi pulled into the school gateway, and I paid my fare before starting the walk up the driveway. The speeches were just finishing, and the families were leaving the marquee to claim their afternoon tea before their children claimed their luggage and their lifts home. I could see the bunting fluttering and the children running towards the tea stalls. Their parents followed less hastily but with similar urgency, the day was still hot, and the drinks were still very much in demand. The ice maker would have been a great asset, and I joined the crowds as they approached the food stalls, large platters of small sandwiches in different flavours, tiered stands of small cakes and patisserie treats, and fruit kebabs were arranged on the tables, parents and children encouraged to help themselves to fuel up ahead of the drive home. The fruit punch was still on offer, and some parents were taking advantage of the tea urns powered by the generator. Everyone was using the washroom facilities, and the associated attendant staff were continually replenishing soap stocks and the rolls of paper in the cubicles, along with the fluffy cotton hand towels. The appearance of these washrooms was of constant cleanliness, the clean water for handwashing was piped in from the school buildings, and the water used to flush the toilets was directed in from the tanker lorries which were parked a short distance away. Dirty water was directed to a separate tanker. I wasn't sure if it would subsequently unload to the school's main sewer, but nothing would happen whilst we had guests. I was astounded by the whole set up. These arrangements certainly took the pressure off the school building and its facilities. That it was possible to stage such a huge event in what was essentially a field was eye-opening for me. I resolved to find out more from Elizabeth about this and saw her ahead of me. She turned and saw me, she stepped towards me smiling, then looked over my shoulder.

'Who's that?'

I turned and saw, halfway up the drive, a figure dressed in dark clothes walking towards us. As I watched the figure draw closer, I could see, with surprise, that Joshua was walking up the drive towards us.

'It's Joshua. Rachel's husband.'

Elizabeth immediately picked up the two-way radio that she had kept clipped to her waistband all day. She pressed a button and spoke quickly, 'Elizabeth calling security to the main drive immediately please.' Almost instantly four of the janitorial team walked through the crowd. They all had earpieces which were relaying the message and they had left their posts beside awnings and generators and hastened to Elizabeth's call. Elizabeth asked them to wait whilst we went to speak to the advancing figure of Joshua who was quite close now. We approached him and could see his determined expression.

'Good afternoon, can we help you?' Elizabeth spoke politely.

'I want to speak to her.' Joshua pointed at me.

Elizabeth kept walking down the drive, and I followed her lead. The security team remained vigilant. Joshua's angry gesture hadn't escaped them. As we passed him, he turned and reached his hand out towards me, similarly to how he had seized hold of me in the hospital. Elizabeth spoke again, but sharply.

'Please don't touch her, we can talk over here.'

Joshua hesitated, then dropped his hand to his side and turned to walk alongside of us. This was an uncomfortable position for him, he would be used to a woman walking behind him. We walked down the drive to the gates.

'We can't ask you to stay, unfortunately. Is there something you wanted to say?'

'I want to know what she is doing. Why is she involving herself with my affairs? She has no business to do so.'

The security team had followed us down the driveway at a distance but were still watching closely. Joshua struck an unusual figure in his long black coat and black trousers. The janitorial staff were all in their knee-length shorts, with several pockets for keys, small tools, their radios and other essential items for their work. Joshua had certainly caught their attention, as had his large dark car, parked at the gateway of the school. Shortly there would be a stream of vehicles all attempting to leave the premises, and he was currently in the way.

'What do you want to know Joshua?' I asked. 'I told you I am Rachel's sister.'

'You are not a true sister to Rachel; her sisters are with their parents. You may look a little like her, but you are definitely not one of the family. You have no rights to see her, no rights to talk to her.'

'That really is Rachel's decision. If she wants me to help her, I will do so. I am worried about her health and want her to get better. We are definitely sisters and I have as much right to see her as anyone else does.'

'NO!' Joshua shouted at me, with the barely concealed anger rising again. 'She is my wife; you will stay away from her!'

Elizabeth turned to him and spoke again, but in a low tone.

'I must ask you to leave now, I hope your wife gets well soon, but you cannot turn up here and abuse my staff.'

She beckoned to the men a dozen or so meters away and they walked swiftly towards us. Joshua saw them and walked to his car.

'I'm going. But stay away from us.'

He glared at me and got into his car. Starting it, he drove quickly across the main road making a U-turn in order to return to the town, causing an oncoming vehicle to brake, and a horn sounded loudly. He disappeared up the road and Elizabeth sighed.

'Right, let's get back to the parents. Are you all right, Mary?'

I nodded and walked back up the driveway, following the security team who were now making their way to the parking areas. They pulled on bright yellow vests and made themselves available to help with loading luggage and directing cars out of the car park, most parents were still enjoying a chat with other families and the tea still being served but a few households, perhaps with longer journeys ahead of them, were starting to load up suitcases and sports bags into cars, arranging them around the feet of tired children and the occasional grandparent who had come along for a lovely day with the family and now found themselves embracing a smelly sports kit, or a bag of shoes, and listening to an excited account of the term, and also of the afternoon just finishing. I returned to the tea tables to assist with any questions or requests for help from any of the families. As I wasn't a member of teaching staff, the pupils would address me as 'Miss' which had been strange to begin with but was something to which I had now adjusted. Parents and visitors didn't address me but could identify me as staff due to the identity badge I was wearing around my neck on a coloured strap. Teachers' badges had red straps and non-teachers wore green straps, so I was easily identifiable. Most parents addressed me by apologising, that they didn't know me but could I ... followed by a request for information or help. I was glad to help people and had some very interesting conversations with some of the families.

Some people were obviously very lucky and had plenty of money to pay huge school fees, and wore lovely clothes, others weren't so wealthy and wore less spectacular clothing, but all were equally focussed on getting a good education for their children. I saw nothing but happy families, although some of the children were by now getting a little tired and emotional. I remained sure that the key to a happy life would be education and was glad that all these children were getting such a good introduction to the wide world of knowledge. I knew that if I allowed any frustration regarding my own early start in life to grow out of control, I would merely reduce further my future opportunities.

Moving on

My possessions had all fitted into a holdall which had been left in the school's lost property for over a year. It was slightly tatty in appearance, no doubt considered as unfashionable by its previous owner but completely serviceable and the right size for my belongings and it should be easy for me to manage on the train. I had acquired little in the way of clothing or possessions since I had arrived at school but had been offered some of the school library books that were to be replaced before the next term. I had accepted a few, one on basic genetics, another on geographical features and a couple more on topics that I had not yet explored. One on planets and another on archaeology - both subjects that I had never encountered before, the Community would not have allowed involvement, even from the point of conversation, in such areas. The belief that the world had been created was at odds with such topics and as such were excluded from the Community school curriculum. I could see that the wider world was a feast for those who wanted to learn, and I was determined to share as much as I could about this. I made sure that my bedroom door was locked and went downstairs to Elizabeth's office.

The big clear up after celebrations day had completed and I would be leaving to get a train to Libby's later. I had arranged to have a last chat with Elizabeth, I hoped that we could remain friends, she had been so helpful to me, and I felt that she and I had formed a bond. I would be having an exit interview with Mrs Higgins before I left too, apparently it would be my chance to offer feedback on my time at Hornbeam House, I couldn't think of anything that I could add to the already efficient and effective working arrangements. The only problem I had encountered had been Sally, and that had been more of an annoyance rather than a problem anyway! Elizabeth was making coffee when I knocked at her door, and we sat at her coffee table for the last time with steaming mugs of frothy coffee. She indicated that I could help myself from a box of biscuits too, but I had enjoyed all the celebratory leftovers so much that it may be a while until I felt like eating much! There had been the usual pastries and fruit offered at breakfast that morning, but I had eaten a banana with a cup of coffee and accepted some pieces of fruit and a couple of wrapped pastries for my lunch which were now in my ancient shoulder bag in my room.

Another person I was to see today, was Rachel. I would call in on her before I caught my train and find out how she was doing. I had thought about what Joshua had said and, whilst I didn't agree with his point of view, I probably would have done had I still been in the Community, and I could understand how he thought he was right. I decided that I should respect him, as Rachel's husband and therefore my brother-in-law, we were now members of the same family. I couldn't allow my newly liberated ways to negatively affect Rachel, especially whilst she was still so unwell. I wanted to make sure she had my telephone number available and could therefore contact me in due course if she wanted to, so I had written it onto a length of ribbon and intended to tie it through one of the buttonholes on her dress should she be still asleep during my visit to the hospital later. She would then have a way to remember my number, as Joshua wouldn't be handling her clothes, that was work done by women.

During my conversation with Mrs Higgins, I spoke about how much I had enjoyed my work at the school and, whilst I had encountered challenges, I had been well-supported in overcoming them. She explained how she would offer a reference for any future employment I may take on, and we agreed that my experience there had been very valuable. I left that meeting with much to reflect on the way that Outsiders had treated me. With the exception of Sally, who I still believed was just too curious for comfort, and Hector, who had demonstrated kindness in the beginning but had sent me the strange messages which had been deemed inappropriate by Elizabeth, the basic courtesy everybody had shown me had been contrary to the warnings given by my parents whilst in the Community; I had received kindness and saw that colourful clothing had not had an impact on my safety or caused any concern to those around me. Collecting my battered shoulder bag and new holdall, I returned my keys, lanyard and identity badge to Elizabeth before accepting a lift from one of the science teachers who was leaving to drive home for the summer.

I got out of the car in the middle of town and made my way to the hospital. I had to see my sister. I retraced the route to Ward Twelve and hoped that Doctor Rowe would be on duty when I arrived. One of the other blue-pyjama-clad staff tracked her down and I was shown to her office where I received an update on Rachel's condition. Doctor Rowe said that Rachel was conscious again and had been in discussions regarding her treatment with the staff. She had repeated her permission for information to be shared with me and her pallor had changed a little, as a result of the transfusion which had reduced the risk of organ damage and the ultimate and insurmountable challenge of organ failure. I walked down the corridor, past huge beds containing almost invisible people, concealed as they were beneath bedclothes, and screened by monitoring machines to which they were wired up and connected to bags of fluid hanging from attached framework. Those patients nearer the doctors' offices seemed to be motionless and I assumed that they were in the same unconscious condition that Rachel had been when she first arrived. As I approached Rachel's bed, now further away from the doctors' offices, I could see that she was no longer lying flat and was plugged into fewer machines although these were still beeping and flashing; she was now awake and turned towards me as I put my shoulder bag and holdall on the floor. I asked if I could sit down, she nodded and smiled.

'Hello, Audrey.'

I reached for her hand, this time it was warmer, and responsive, less like the bird that had come to mind on my first visit.

'You look so much better; Rachel I was so very worried about you. What have the doctors said?'

She replied that they were investigating the cause of a problem with her blood, there seemed to be two possibilities; that it was a rare type of cancer, or possibly due to an infection somewhere in her body. More tests needed to be done, and in fact a lot of blood tests had already been carried out on the samples taken when she had first arrived at hospital, before the transfusion had been done. She felt better for the transfusion, although she had not yet told Joshua about it. She wasn't sure how to approach the problem of communicating this with Joshua. We discussed how she felt about her situation. She said that being in hospital had made her realise the importance of her health. And the absence of Community members had allowed her to think carefully about what she wanted to do with her life. That she had seen me a few times and seen that I was well and independent had added to her thoughts. She asked me what was happening in my life, I told her about my job at the school. I told her that I had a different job to go to and I would be staying with a friend in the meantime. She asked how I had come to the point of wanting to leave, and she wanted to know what my long-term plan was. Letting go of my hand she reached out and touched my hair.

'You look so different. You look happy. I'm frightened for what may become of you. The wickedness that you have been exposed to, how can it work out well?'

I took her hand again in both of mine. 'Rachel, what happens in the Community isn't always right, I can see now that there were things going on that were very wrong. Now, I can choose what happens to me. I will still get married, I will still have children, but I will choose who I marry, and I will choose when to have children. Also, I will choose how many children I will have. So many people have been kind, so many people have helped me. Not all of the Community people are good people.'

'I know, Audrey. I have had time to think, and I want to think more about what I should do.' She looked at my bags. 'Where are you going?' She looked at me intently.

I told her I would be staying with the friends who had helped me first of all, and eventually going to my new job later in the summer. Rachel told me that she was likely to be in hospital for another week, but then she would be sent home but kept under medical supervision whilst her blood situation was examined. Any treatment would follow, and she was likely to have many more appointments over the summer. I asked about Joshua. Rachel could only say that he seemed to be a good man, but she had only met him once before her marriage to him. Our father had given his permission for her to be married, and she had accepted Joshua as was the normal process in the Community. Their home was a house that belonged to one of Joshua's uncles and Joshua was trying to establish himself with a business of his own. If he couldn't do that, he would be forever an employee in the businesses of his brothers, cousins and, eventually, the rest of the Community.

Similar to my own father, I realised, who was a worker bee merely contributing to the business owners' wealth and never likely to achieve wealth of his own or the status of a business owner. I could understand, now, the determination felt by Joshua. If he wanted to have any sort of recognition within his Community, he would need status as a successful, wealthy business owner. Only then could he, or his future sons, ever have any hope of reaching the status of an elder, or a Senior Man. One successful family would be matched with another. The hierarchy worked that way and the powerful became more powerful and the weaker, beholden families became more trapped by their own situation where they had had to borrow money from wealthier members to enable them to be able to buy the required detached houses. I could now realise the pressure that could be felt by Joshua, and with Rachel unable to keep house for him he would be staying with his parents. Poor health was often regarded as a punishment and therefore sympathy and support would be unlikely to be offered from the Community. If Rachel was going to need a series of appointments and care, she would need support and I wondered how well Joshua could do that.

I asked Rachel if she had let our parents know of her illness. She hadn't. I asked if she wanted to return to Joshua's house after her hospital stay, or would she consider going to stay with our parents? She said she wouldn't go to our parents but said nothing about going home to Joshua. We discussed her situation, and I explained that she would need some help in taking care of herself and wondered how likely Joshua would be to help her. She said nothing. I asked her if his family would help her, and she went pale. Silent, fat tears leaked out of her eyes and slid down her face in an almost constant stream. After a few minutes of this quiet misery, she rubbed her face, took a deep breath and said that she didn't think they would be very helpful.

'We need to think about this, Rachel,' I said. 'We have to get you better.'

She nodded, the tears had stopped, but the sadness on her face was awful to see.

'Shall we talk to the doctor?' More nodding.

I walked down to the office to ask if Doctor Rowe was available to talk. She wasn't but would join us as soon as she became available. I wondered if I could find someone else to look after Rachel. I would be staying with Libby for a few weeks, and I didn't have any transport, so it would be difficult to take Rachel for her appointments. I sent a message asking Libby if I could chat with her as soon as she was free. She rang me immediately and as soon as I pressed the green button I heard her voice, higher than usual due to anxiety, I thought.

'Are you all right?'

I said I was and explained that I might be looking for someone who could look after Rachel for the next few weeks, and would that be something that Libby could help with? Would there be someone in the network who would be close enough to a hospital to help out? I said that I would pay for Rachel's expenses and said that I wasn't sure of her feelings about leaving the Community. Libby said she would make a couple of calls and message me back. I returned to Rachel, and we talked some more, I spoke of life outside the Community and asked the most direct question I could ever ask my sister. Would she consider leaving the Community?

Getting better

Boarding the train later that afternoon, I sat in a window seat at a table which would accommodate four passengers. One seat was already occupied when I sat down, and I thought over the afternoon's discussions. Rachel had agreed that she may consider leaving the Community, and Libby had found a household in Market Wenton that had agreed to help her if necessary. This would be a huge step for Rachel, as far as I knew she had had no ideas of leaving before – but, she would have probably said that about me until I left, wouldn't she? It had taken longer at the hospital than I had anticipated, and the discussion with Doctor Rowe had been very helpful, but rather complex. Apparently, Rachel could be treated at another hospital, but I would need to confirm her new address so that the notes could be transferred to the new hospital and arrange for someone to collect her from the hospital on her day of discharge. I resolved to do that and would try to see what could be done with the people in Market Wenton. I knew that there was a small hospital in Market Wenton, which should make it easy for Rachel to access her treatment and consider her future plans.

I hauled my holdall up off the seat beside me and on to my lap as a red-faced man approached. His face looked rather cross, and I felt he wasn't likely to be chatty. My tatty shoulder bag was on the table in front of me, so I was rather squashed under all this luggage. He sat down with a grunt, without looking at me. He put a laptop bag on the table, casting a faintly disgusted look at my scruffy luggage. I ignored him and looked out of the window as the train gathered speed and the buildings started to flash past the windows. I was lost in thought, considering how the last few months had gone, and what form the ones ahead may take when I realised that my holdall was sliding off my leg. I shifted it a bit, but that seemed to make no difference, something was still sliding off my leg… I looked down and saw that the red-faced man had slid his hand under the table and was stroking my leg just above my knee. He slid his hand up my thigh slightly and started to squeeze the fleshier part of my leg. Suddenly, all the rage I had felt when I had been in the Community meetings, where other men had stood too close, erupted inside my head.

'Please take your hand off my leg, RIGHT NOW!'

I didn't ever remember shouting before, ever in my life. Heads turned. People looked. The hand stopped squeezing. The world stood still for a minute, and a woman from the seats adjacent spoke.

'I think you'd better sit somewhere else'.

I started to gather my shoulder bag into my bundle of luggage.

'No, not you, love. HIM.'

She pointed at the red-faced man who was smirking.

'I don't know what she's on about. She's mad. An attention-seeking bitch'.

I felt my face get red now, 'You were squeezing my leg. Get away from me.'

By now there were several women looking at him, and a couple of men from a nearby table stood up.

'I think it's time you moved to another table, mate, don't you?'

Seeing that there was a rather hostile crowd around us, the smirk disappeared, and he grabbed his laptop bag, stood up and walked down the corridor.

'Bloody psycho bitch. You'll be in trouble one day!'

I heard someone call out, 'On your way mate, on your way. We don't need people like you here.'

One of the women stood in the corridor beside my table.

'Are you all right love? Did he do anything else?'

I shook my head, and to my rage I felt tears run down my face.

'No, I'm really fine. He just squeezed my leg.'

Another woman joined in. 'There's no JUST about it, it's not his leg to touch. Maybe I'll put my bag on that seat, give you a bit of space. Would you mind if I sat opposite?'

I shook my head, and she put her own holdall, rather smarter than mine, on the seat and sat opposite her bag. The only other occupant of the table, an elderly man who had been asleep since before I sat down, shifted slightly but continued his doze. He sat slightly slumped in his seat, with his head leaned against the window, cushioned by a folded sweater he appeared to be very comfortable. The other people who had stood to challenge the squeezing man one by one caught my eye, offering a thumbs up signal or words of encouragement, I was urged to Stay Cool Sister, to be Right On and I agreed that I was OK, Fine and that everything was All Good. The lady sitting down introduced herself as Gloria. She didn't look much older than me but said that her own daughter would have reacted the same way as I had, and that I should be proud of myself. I blurted out that she didn't look old enough to have a daughter and she laughed.

'It's the Nigerian heritage, girl, we have amazing skin.'

I mumbled an apology.

'Hey, never apologise for complimenting someone! We may not look the same, be the same age, or live the same lives, but we're all good, strong women and we need to stand against bad treatment. No one can touch what isn't theirs. Good for you for calling him out.'

I began to relax. This lady was entirely right. I thought of Rachel. I would definitely stand against bad treatment. She deserved to get well, and then to make her own decisions.

Arriving at the station in Market Wenton, I hauled my holdall and shoulder bag up steps, along walkways and down to the station entrance. I made my way to the car park and looked around for Libby. She was running down towards me from the far side of the parking area and her face was beaming.

'Mary, Hi! You look so well, let me carry that. How was your journey? I've spoken to the couple I mentioned. We can visit them now if you'd like. What a busy time you've had. How are you doing?'

Once I had answered all these questions, we had reached the car, and Libby drove us out onto the main road to visit the couple.

'How do you know these people, Libby? Rachel needs quite a lot of care and understanding. Would they be able to help her?'

'They are members of the Network; I know they have helped other people. The husband works at the local hospital, he's an administration manager there, and they have a small child, so the wife works at home, she makes celebration cakes for people wanting them for weddings and parties. Rachel will be well looked after, and you can visit her whenever you want to. What's her situation?'

I started to explain, and Libby was listening as she drove. The whole story took some time, and I was only about halfway through when she pulled up outside a small house, switched the engine off and suggested we met with Matthew and Agnes. Waiting on the doorstep having pressed the bell, I looked around the front garden, it wasn't too different from Rachel's current property, and I hoped she would like it here.

The house was joined to another house, which would be a new experience for her, and there was a small white car parked on the driveway. As the door opened, I turned and looked straight into the smiling face of a blonde lady who was holding the hand of a small boy who seemed anxious to return to somewhere else, he was tugging at her hand and saying 'Mumm-mmmeee, mummm-mmeeeEEE,' she beckoned us in and we followed her through a doorway where there was a range of toy cars and trucks scattered over the floor, the boy immediately resumed his play and lay on the floor pushing the cars and trucks all the time keeping up a chattering commentary describing what the trucks were doing, where they were going and what they were saying to each other. We sat on a small squashy sofa and Agnes went to bring us cups of coffee. Returning with a tray laden with coffee cups and a large cafetiere she sat down and, addressing me directly, asked what I could tell her about Rachel. As we drank our coffee, I mentioned her treatment that would need to take place, that Agnes assured me wouldn't be a problem, they had transport so could drive her if she wasn't fit to walk. I spoke of a sensitive family situation, and Agnes interrupted.

'Is she in the Community? We left a few years ago, a year before we got married, as we wanted to be together but were destined to marry other people. We understand that she may find adjusting a problem. Will she be leaving for good?'

'I hope so, but it must be her decision. I don't think her husband's family treat her very well. She has a blood disorder which is being diagnosed. I'm hoping she will get better soon and spend some time considering her options. Our parents are hardworking, but lowly and our options were limited. I am not in touch with our parents yet, I have tried but they were angry. I'll try again and sort things out for Rachel before I leave for Tamford. I'll be starting work there in August.'

Agnes nodded, she offered to show me the room which would be Rachel's. I followed her up the stairs to a room overlooking the rear garden. There was a single bed, a table and chair and a chest of drawers. It was quite plain in its decoration and had thick pillows and a deep mattress under a quilt on the bed and a big fluffy comforter folded up at the end. There was a small side table beside the wooden headboard, with a lamp. I could see that Rachel would feel quite safe here and would be able to relax. Agnes showed me the bathroom beside Rachel's room, and the child's room opposite that. I looked into the room as she opened the door. It was a light room, with a soft green carpet on the floor. A shelf unit held some colourful plastic toys, and the small bed had a collection of cuddly animals arranged on it. I could see another shelf on which was a stack of colourful books. There were a few toys on the floor, and some clothes scattered about but it looked clean, and the sunlight streamed in through the window. Rachel's room faced the other way, but would probably get the morning sunshine, I thought. A further closed door I presumed to be the parents' room and we descended the stairs returning to the living room to find the little boy showing Libby his green truck and demonstrating how the back part of it could 'tip out the muck'. He looked up as Agnes returned and gleefully told her that Libby had been playing Traffic with him. Libby was sitting on the floor amongst the trucks and cars and seemed to be enjoying herself.

We took our leave of Agnes, and the truck-loving Henry, and started the drive back to Libby's house. I told her of the job in Tamford and she was keen to hear about the family. She suggested that we drive over there to visit before I started the job, and I agreed that it was a good idea. By now it was dinner time, and our stomachs noisily reminded us of that as we drove onto the driveway outside Libby's house. She unlocked the front door, and I hauled in my holdall which thudded onto the hall floor. She laughed and directed me upstairs to the room I had used before and I unpacked my bag, separating the clothes that needed to be laundered away from the ones that were merely creased. I went for a quick shower, it had been a warm day, and I felt a bit grubby after my encounter with the red-faced man on the train. I put different jeans on and went downstairs to Libby. She was just taking a pizza out of the oven, and we sat at the table where I had sat for my first breakfast all those weeks ago. I no longer felt the need to give thanks for the food on my plate, but I did appreciate the effort that went in to providing my meals. I no longer believed that it was granted by a god of any name, but by the skill and effort of endless workers within a chain of agriculture and commerce. And Libby of course.

Sitting with Libby and Brian in their living room later, sipping chilled white wine, I mused on the last few months. A lot had happened, and I was looking forward to the next few weeks before I left for Tamford. Libby had finished her term's teaching and we would be arranging a visit to Michael and Grace in the next few weeks. I needed to check that all my clothes were suitable for my new job, and now that I had passed my driving test, Libby had offered to include me on her car insurance and was happy for me to drive her car over to Market Wenton to visit Rachel once she had made her move. I hadn't had time to have the motorway lessons before I had left, so would arrange to have these as soon as my licence arrived at Libby's house. To be able to use Libby's car was an extra bonus, and Libby had suggested that she drive me down to collect Rachel when she was discharged from the hospital. I decided to telephone Ward Twelve the following day to let them know of Rachel's new accommodation and the name of the hospital. I hoped that I would be able to speak to her, I wanted to tell her about Agnes.

Retiring to bed that evening, I changed into my pyjamas, and went through my now-usual routine of skincare and hair brushing before getting into bed and lying in the place where I had begun my new life. It had been less than three months since I had left my first life. How quickly I had adapted to life outside the Community, I looked different, thought differently and, although I believed that I had not changed my personality, I behaved differently. Life had improved for me – I had a job, I had learned to swim, drive, study and to make friends. I had a reasonable amount of money in a bank account and felt as if I had become truly alive since I was now able to make all my own decisions. I thought about my father. How he had reacted when I telephoned him. Of Rachel, how ill she was and how she would need help to overcome her current situation. Of my mother. How she struggled to look after all of her children, how I now felt she was mistaken in her approach to my poor sister, and how badly she had been treated in the past. I also thought of the ways in which Community members had treated each other. In the last three months I had been able to walk around, without needing to check whether I had been seen, whether I needed to moderate my appearance, behaviour or speech. This would not have happened before, and I remembered noticing that some of the cars I had seen on my flight from that final church meeting had contained Community members. If either of the two men who had run after me had caught up with me, the consequences for me would have been significant. I could only guess at the effect on my parents – my father's anger when I had telephoned had confirmed that great shame and hardship would have landed onto the family. I realised that I hadn't spoken to Rachel about that, and she had married shortly after I had left. I wondered if the poor treatment she had endured from Joshua's parents was because of my action. Although I now knew that no blame that could be attached to me; it was a result of contorted thinking and isolation techniques that meant anyone who spoke to an Outsider was ostracised. I could now see that the created dependencies within the Community were a way of forcing members together. The deep purpose of isolating the Community members was still slightly confusing to me – I had seen that nothing bad had happened to me since I had left, I had had that unpleasant encounter on the train earlier in the day, but that had been no worse than what had happened to some girls and women within the Community at the hands of Community men and in the presence of Community members. I knew that there were no bad situations that could affect me, as long as I remained mentally strong. Whilst in the Community I had needed strength, but that was to deal with the treatment from the other Community members. I had had to concentrate on my behaviour and appearance to ensure that I remained in line with Community beliefs and restrictions. Now, I could concentrate on broadening my education and expanding my mind. I must have fallen asleep whilst thinking and remembering all this, because suddenly there was bright light on the bedroom ceiling and the sound of birdsong entering through the bedroom window.

I remembered that this was the first day after my job at the school, and the day I was to telephone Rachel to confirm her move to her new life.

Going forward

Standing at the kitchen window, a cup of coffee in one hand, my phone in the other, I listened as the call rang out. There was a crowd of small birds around the bird feeders hanging in the lilac tree about thirty feet outside the window. I watched as the little birds flew to the feeders, took a seed, or beak full of food away deeper into the tree. There were smaller birds in the branches around the feeders, and there seemed to be a constant rotation of birds coming from the centre of the tree, fluttering and hopping along to the feeders and taking their spoils to eat in private, or to share with juveniles. I watched as the parent birds hurried back and forth to their young; the insistent chirping of the sleek, stationary smaller birds contrasted somewhat with the slightly unpreened appearance of the harassed-looking parent birds, with no time to spend on sprucing their own feathers, their dishevelled appearance reminded me of my mother. She would spend all her time maintaining the house and garden – edible plants only were grown, plants grown for purely decorative purposes were frowned upon and whispers would soon start amongst the other women if anyone dared to indulge in such practices. Decoration was seen as sinful indulgence, and ensured that the Community members wore plain, unpatterned clothing, with no jewellery, cosmetics or hairstyling. My mother enjoyed working with her plants, wearing her customary dark clothing, she was well camouflaged in her garden and seemed to benefit from the calmness in the sunshine and the breeze.

'Hello?' I returned to the present. Dr Rowe had answered the phone and sounded slightly breathless. I introduced myself and started to explain about the plans I had made for Rachel.

'Mary, we are really short for time, Joshua is here and he's trying to take Rachel away. Security have called the police and we are trying to calm the situation. We need Rachel to stay here for another couple of days, if we can prevent Joshua from influencing her.'

I could hear shouting in the background, and bangs, which could have been a door slamming. I asked if I should call back, but Dr Rowe answered hastily.

'No. no, I can take the address of the hospital she will attend, then I should go back to see what is happening.'

I stated the address of the Market Wenton Hospital and gave Matthew's name as Rachel's main contact. I hung up the call, after saying that I would collect Rachel the day after tomorrow. This gave me enough time to go and buy Rachel some clothes, a pair of pyjamas, some long sleeved tops and a pair of loose trousers and a wrap-around skirt, as well as some underwear and a pair of lace-up shoes and some house slippers would allow her to settle at Agnes and Matthew's house whilst she considered her future. I knew that she would need space to think, and time to recover from her illness. I would visit her and pay for her upkeep until she decided whether she would leave the Community and become eligible for assistance from the Network or return to her life with Joshua and the Community. Libby had given me a certificate saying that I was covered by insurance whilst driving her car, and I would have the freedom of being able to drive myself to visit Rachel. I had a few weeks to go before I would leave for my new job in Tamford, and in that time I hoped that Rachel would be able to make her decision. I was looking forward to spending time with her, and Libby too. I had grown so much as a person, and intellectually too, in the weeks I had been away from my family. I might learn more about them from Rachel, I was keen to get news from her and find out if she had anything to say about the treatment of our two younger sisters.

Driving down the main roads on the way to collect Rachel a couple of days later, Libby spoke of the way the Network operated. Apparently, there would be some money available to Rachel for her fresh start if that was her decision. As she hadn't actually said that she wanted to leave the Community, but her actions indicated that she would be doing so, big decisions could not be made. Once she was feeling a bit better, and had time to think and decide, the Network could take over but until then I would cover her costs. I had brought some of the new clothes with us, so that she could leave hospital with some dignity – I knew that she wouldn't have worn trousers before, so this would be a big change for her. I was looking forward to seeing her, and Libby was too. Brian hadn't accompanied us, and we would drive Rachel straight to Matthew and Agnes's house.

We drove into the hospital car park, and I checked that we had the right coins to pay for our ticket on our departure – I hoped that it wouldn't be too long; walking past the reception desk, we followed the green line to Ward Twelve for what we hoped would be the final time. We arrived at Ward Twelve and pressed a buzzer to gain admittance. A blue-clad, masked figure opened the door for us and conducted us to the office where I had met Dr Rowe before. Asking us to wait, the anonymous person left, and we sat in the quiet atmosphere of the office. We could hear the bleeping of machines and occasional footsteps as they hastened along the corridor. After a few minutes, more footsteps approached and this time the door opened. Dr Rowe entered, taking her mask off as she did so.

'Hello. Thank you for coming, it has been a tricky couple of days, but we are ready for Rachel's next step.'

Dr Rowe explained that Joshua had been spoken to by the police regarding his behaviour at the hospital and they hadn't seen him since his outburst. The buzzer system had been connected as a man had arrived the day before, demanding to see Rachel, and when she had seen him, her fearful and panic-stricken reaction had led the staff to ask him to leave. It turned out that he was Joshua's father and Rachel feared that he would try to force her to leave. She had said little more to the staff but had insisted that she was happy to leave with me and they were supporting her in this. The buzzer allowed the staff to assess any unexpected visitors and it was likely to be disconnected once Rachel had left. I handed over my battered shoulder bag, containing Rachel's new clothes and Dr Rowe asked us to wait for a minute. Libby and I looked at each other. This was not a nice situation for anyone connected, we both knew that the Community would try anything to keep members out of the public eye, or away from any sort of external authority. Investigations into the way of Community life were unwelcome and we understood the desperation of Joshua's family. On the other hand, if Rachel did leave the Community, it was likely that she would be cut off once and for all. The door opened again, and Dr Rowe returned, followed by a thin woman in oversized clothing, but with a smile on her face and carrying my tatty shoulder bag. Rachel looked so different now, in her new clothes. She had opted for a long-sleeved blue t-shirt, and trousers in a colour somewhere between sand and oatmeal. Her shoes looked better, I had remembered that she took the same size in shoes as I did, so they did seem to fit properly. Looking at her face, the blue colour of her eyes seemed extra bright and was accentuated by the colour of her t-shirt. Her expression was rather apprehensive, which was quite understandable given her recent experiences, and I asked her if she was ready. She nodded, accepted a cardboard envelope from Dr Rowe before handing me my bulging shoulder bag. Dr Rowe explained that an appointment had been made for Rachel to attend Market Wenton Hospital on the coming Friday and she should attend to establish her treatment and reviews. All the necessary records had been sent directly to the hospital; the folder just contained information that may be helpful to Rachel. Then Dr Rowe pressed a button on the wall and spoke into a small grille beneath it 'Porter to Ward Twelve please. Porter to Ward Twelve!' She asked Rachel to get into a wheelchair beside the double doors, settling her in with her cardboard folder securely tucked onto her lap with the shoulder bag on top of it, and stated that it was quite normal for a patient to be accompanied to their transport on departing hospital care, particularly when the patient was not yet back to full fitness. I also thought that it would also be useful in case there was anyone outside the hospital who may be looking for Rachel. Libby and I would be glad of any support, should that be the case. I felt that Joshua and his father may possibly try to influence Rachel again but hoped that we would be able to leave without incident. I asked Rachel if she wanted to leave a contact number for Joshua, as he was her husband, and it seemed a bit mean to just vanish. She agreed that Dr Rowe could offer my telephone number as a point of contact, should Joshua ask the hospital for it, and we would write a letter to him after a couple of days, offering reassurance of her safety and outlining her situation.

A young man arrived, wearing a grey t-shirt with PORTER printed in orange letters across the chest and, as he turned, I could see that it was printed on the back too. He greeted Rachel and then me and Libby. Thanking Dr Rowe for all her help and kindness we set off, following the green line again, as we returned to Libby's car. We chatted with the porter, he related some of the funny incidents that happened during his typical working day, and we enjoyed his company. He carefully and gently helped Rachel into Libby's car, she wanted to sit in the back seat, so she settled in as I went to pay for the parking ticket. I was walking back from the machine when I noticed Joshua's car driving into the car park. He seemed to be looking for a space to park and I didn't think he had noticed me, surrounded as I was with other people trying to work out the machinations of the ticket payment system. I made my way back to Libby's car, trying to keep a low profile. I got in just as she was starting the engine and said that he was nearby. Rachel went white, and I told her to turn away from the windows, the rear windows of Libby's car were dark-tinted so the likelihood of her being recognised was low, unless someone was very close to the car – which could happen in a car park. I knew that Joshua wouldn't recognise Libby, but he might recognise me. Libby indicated some clutter that was in the footwell in front of me – I grabbed a baseball hat and crammed it onto my head quickly, and then seized some sunglasses which were folded up in a cupholder beside the gear lever. She flipped down the sun visor, and I did to the one on my side of the car too. I focussed my gaze on the handbrake and Libby drove towards the car park exit, pausing only to feed the ticket into the slot beside the barrier, which raised jerkily as she reached for the button to close the window. Just then I heard a gasp from Rachel as a voice near to the car could be heard quite clearly.

'I don't know, I couldn't get to see her yesterday, but we will try again now. No...'

The window closed at that point, and I knew that Rachel had recognised Joshua's voice, as I had too. Libby moved the car forwards, and we turned out of the car park, driving back towards the main roads and thus to take Rachel to the beginning of what could be her new life. It was her choice, and to have that option was exactly what she had not had for over twenty years. Choice. Something that was taken for granted by so many, available to more than they believed, due to the exact social conditions imposed on them by their communities or families, or both, and a right to everyone. Education had allowed me to come to this understanding, and the time away from a controlling environment. With these two options now available to Rachel, I hoped that she would be able to come to a decision of her own. Choice should not be taken from anyone. Freedom is a right for everyone and, as we drove through the sunshine, past the industrial areas of the outskirts of the town where I had learned so much about myself and the wider world, away from Rachel's most recent isolation and towards the wide roads that would take us back to the small towns only a few miles from where we had grown up, believing our world was limited and surrounded by fear, I began to relax as the distance behind the car grew. Libby was returning to her happy home, I was returning to my future, and Rachel was travelling to discover what could be her future.

Sequel to Vanishing Point

Valuable Perspective follows Mary's new life as she begins her job in a new city, how has Rachel fared since leaving hospital? What about their sisters? Can the lessons learned in early life be forgotten? Is Mary right to continue with her thirst for learning? How can the past be prevented from poisoning the future?

www.colin-saxo.com   colin@colin-saxo.com

Printed in Great Britain
by Amazon